Antonio Ventura • Francesco Dicarlo
Giacomo Carito • Silvano Trevisani • Mario De Marco

The guide-book of Apulia

Historico-artistic itinerary

Capone Editore

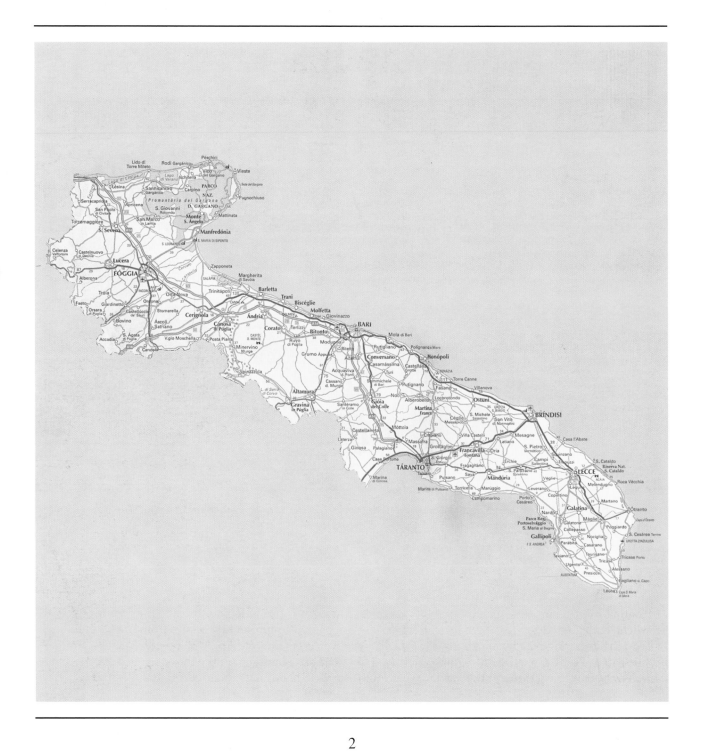

Apulia

Apulia is a charming land of ancient souls where for many centuries a lot of civilizations of the Mediterranean Sea and Europe have alternated with each other and stratified leaving their indelible mark. Then, when in the 16th century, political and economical interests were already concerned with Atlantic routes, the extreme ramification of Italy became a peripheral area and it was no more the meeting-point of history. Only in the 18th century there was the beginning of the rediscovery, on the part of historical travellers, of the beauty of monuments and nature of our land, of its people, of events and traditions which today scholars try to revive and restore with spreading studies too.

The aim of this guide-book is to point out beauties and monuments which represent the pride even of small municipalities. But we must remember that, just for the extreme work of synthesis, the reader will have to consult deeper and more specialized studies' books in order to satisfy his/her interests and curiosity. Skimming through the pages of this book, where the narration proceeds together with so many figures, we will find out the traces and the witnesses which our ancestors have left us since the prehistory and so we will be able to make ideal journeys in the Stone Age and that of terramare, among those who raised mysterious megalithic monuments, dolmen, menhir and specchie (mounds). Then we will meet the mythical Dauni, Peucezi and Messapian, people from Magna Graecia and the Romans. We can easily suppose that just in the territory of Apulia Christianity arrived, before reaching Europe, of which remain the ruins of the most ancient temples of our religion, which in the Middle Ages bore witness to the flourishing of the rupestrian (rocky) civilization of Byzantine monachism which has handed down such wonderful icons. Then arrived the Longobards, the Franks, the Arabs, the Normans, the Angevins, afterwards the Swabians and the Spaniards, and by these rulers, who were the forefathers themselves of today's people from Apulia, were raised, also changed according to local sensitivity, magnificent monuments, churches, convents, towers, castles and palaces in Romanesque, Gothic, Renaissance and Baroque styles with so many local varieties and features. Even in the popular and rustic architecture we can find the signs of the people who settled in Apulia, where, as it is said in this book, memory wants to claim the role of its presence not only to take again possession of so many identities, but also as cultural and economical resource to be committed to future generations.

Mario De Marco

The province of Foggia

The Abbey of Santa Maria of Pulsano

«Anthology of the world», as Capitanata has often been defined for the rich landscape of this area and the complexity of its history, which blend together creating a harmony of environment, culture and traditions: going there means living an exalting adventure among new and various colours, emotions and sensations.

The journey to the lands of Dauni can start from Gargano, being, from time immemorial, destination for travellers: before, Classical people came here to get good omens from the mysterious Gods of the place; then, during the Middle Ages, the worship for St. Michele went on attracting crowds of people along the "Via Sacra Langobardorum", once destination for princes, popes and crusaders, today a fixed route for pious "companies" of pilgrims. Proceeding along it means learning the deep mysticism of some sanctuaries among the most important ones of Capitanata: St. Maria of Ripalta, St. Nazario, St. Maria of Stignano, St. Matteo, St. Giovanni Rotondo, Monte St. Angelo, St. Maria and St. Leonardo of Siponto, Madonna dell'Incoronata (the Crowned Virgin).

For a long time the Headland has had a difficult access for lack of suitable streets till the opening of the railway station San Severo-Peschici, in 1931 and the

Zagare Bay

development of the coastal road, well connected with the motorway entries of Poggio Imperiale, San Severo and Foggia, proved to be successful to break this isolation. Today there is no inaccessible place and this condition emphasizes the most extraordinary natural resources of Italy: the continuous succession of over 130 kilometres of beaches, coves, bays, cliffs, short sandy shores, suggestive villages on the rocks, surprising archaeological remains, ancient abbeys now represent a fixed chapter of the guide-books of international tourism.

From Gargano we can reach Tavoliere, the cradle of ancient civilizations, so called from "tabulae censuales": the contracts drawn up by Roman censors with those who rent the pastures for the flocks of Sannio, Abruzzo, Irpinia. The sheep went down the plains of Apulia following the route of "tractoria" mentioned by codes of Teodosio and Justinian; along these ways of transhumance, which after that became 111 metres wide, up to the 19th century the herds continuously went from mountains to plains, varying their exit according to the liturgical dates of the worship for St. Michele: from 29th September to 8th May. And the great

Rocchetta Sant'Antonio

commerce of the products of stock-raising was regulated by Alfonso I from Aragon who created the "Regia Dogana della Mena delle Pecore" (the Royal Customs of sheep trade), used to control the access of cattle in the "leaseholds" of Tavoliere, after the payment of "fida" (land let for grazing).

From 1447 to 1865 the landscape and the agrarian history of the Dauni's countryside were conditioned and immobilized by this economic-administrative institution; then it was up to the unitary State to remove the archaic pastoral structure and pave the way for the cultural transformation which has had its fundamental stages in the construction of Apulian Aqueduct, in Fascist reclamation and in the recent modernization of local agriculture.

The last stage in Capitanata is in the Dauno Subappennines, with luxuriant vegetation and rich in small streams of spring-waters in the enchanting scenery of mountains, from which delightful villages rich in history and art appear. Nevertheless, among these hilly glacises and mountainous ravines, there are still a small and slow economy and a land reduced to pow-

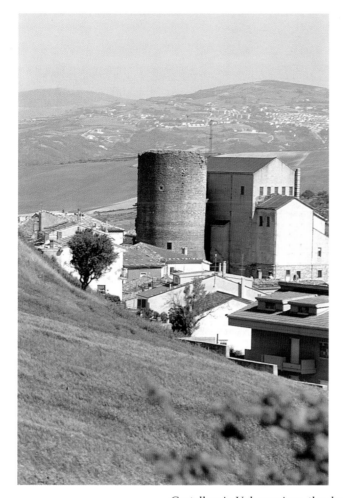

Castelluccio Valmaggiore, the donjon, and the rampart in Lucera

der being inadequate to feed many families: the only remedy for such lack of resources was, till some time ago, the migration into the most unexpected places of the five Continents, hence the drastic demographic decrease. However, travelling through the Dauno Subappennines means meeting with the signs of stone left by the proud power of the illustrious feudal families: in Lucera the castle with its Angevin towers; in Troia the Guelph cathedral in the really pure Romanesque style of Apulia; in Bovino the ducal palace with the Norman tower supported by a massive pyramid-shaped buttress; in Orsara the seat of the Knights of Calatrava; in St. Agata of Apulia, the medieval fortress in its typical quadrangular structure.

Gargano and Tremiti Islands

A monolithic block rich in millenary history, a

Monte Sant'Angelo, the cave of St. Michele

series of monuments, a rich archaeological heritage and, above all, a nature where the various suggestions of Italy's landscapes blend each other: all this is Gargano. The only person who really knows it is the Archangel Michele. He has been living here for fifteen centuries, exactly since the 8th May 493, date of His apparition before an astonished shepherd of the place just called Gargano.

The choice of this district on the part of the heavenly visitor was not by chance: he avoided the coastlines as if He foresaw the future mess and, on the contrary, He chose the inaccessible bulwark of Monte St. Angelo. Therefore, those who want to see the Headland in its true spiritual essence will have to leave the coastal road and after some effort to go along the bends of the road surrounding the sides of the mountain, in search of that wild nature which charmed the Archangel too. After reaching the top, the view of the landscape below will be wonderful: the wide Sipontina plain studded with olive-trees and farmhouses, and, on the horizon, the wide blue surface of the sea. Nevertheless, we will become familiar

Monte Sant'Angelo, the entrance to the Basilica ant the bell tower

with Gargano's secrets when we enter the district, destination, starting from the 6th century, along the "Via Sacra Langobardorum", of that deep tradition of pilgrimages, being kept alive till today.

Of great suggestion is the monumental structure of Palatina Basilica, inside which the marble statue of St. Michele attributed to Andrea Sansovino sparkles. Near to the imposing octagonal bell tower, ordered to be built in 1274 by Charles I d'Angiò, there is the access to the Sanctuary through two portals: the right-side one is by Simeone from Monte St. Angelo (1395);

the other one is only a nineteenth-century imitation. A staircase winds from them and reaches the Romanesque entrance created for Guiscardo's wish: its bronze shutters, gift from the noble Pantaleone III from Amalfi, were melted in Costantinopoli in 1076 and on the two leaves twenty-four window-panes were built representing scenes from the Old and New Testament and the Apparition of St. Michele before St. Lorenzo Maiorano. In the inside of the church various artistic hand-manufactured objects of great value are worth seeing: the walnut sculptured stalls of the capi-

Monte Sant'Angelo, the Swabian-Angevin-Aragonese Castle

tular choir; the chapel of relics; the altar in Seicento style devoted to St. Francesco and the others to St. Pietro, Christ Crucified and Archangel.

After going out of Sanctuary Cave, we can go up to the Swabian-Aragonese Castle, protected by massive ramparts among which there is the mighty Tower of Giants. From its ancient walls, once residence of the lords of "Honor Montis Sancti Angeli" it is possible to cast a glance either at the history, or at the nature: on one side the church of St. Mary the Greater, the Tomb of Rotari, not a sepulchre but a baptistery of the 12th century, the churches of St. Benedetto, St. Anthony the Abbot, St. Apollinare, the ex-convent of St. Francesco of the 14th century, now seat of the Museum of arts and popular traditions of Gargano "Giovanni Tancredi" and the spontaneous architecture of medieval quarter "Junno"; on the opposite side, instead, a thrilling and charming landscape of gorges and valleys, on which small villages surrounding a donjon or a fortress such as: Carpino, Ischitella, Vico appear like grips clung on rocky precipices...

After passing Monte St. Angelo, we can begin the

San Giovanni Rotondo, Santa Maria delle Grazie and the small cell of Father Pius

San Marco in Lamis, the Convent of St. Matteo

real adventure in the unspoilt nature of Gargano after short stages in the Abbey of Santa Maria of Pulsano, in San Giovanni Rotondo where the "venerable" Father Pius from Pietralcina lies, in San Marco in Lamis and in the Sanctuary of Stignano, in the ruins of Castelpagano and the neolithic Cave of Paglicci in the neighbourhood of Rignano.

A suggestive place is Bosco Quarto, on the slopes of Mount Spigno, a thousand metres high; but we will meet the real wood only in "Umbra Wood" situated in the centre of the massif. It is impossible not to be impressed by the almost sacred majesty of the place: huge ivy-mantled beeches, imposing Turkey oaks, thick undergrowth and, in the half light, roebucks, beech-martens, badfers, foxes, wild boars. The vegetation is also full of a rich avifauna such as: woodpigeons, jays, sparrows while in the glades, kestrels and buzzards fly about in search of reptiles and rodents.

When we leave the green paradise of Umbra Wood, in the place of its small lakes and myriads of paths we will meet the charming coastal landscape sometimes interrupted by the ancient lookout towers

Vieste (*above*) and Peschici

built by local population against Dalmatian pirates and barbaric corsairs...

From San Menaio, situated in a wonderful green dell of pine-woods and orange-groves, to Rodi, heir to mythical Uria and seat of the Romanesque Sanctuary devoted to Madonna della Libera, the coastline is a continuous series of astonishing corners: twisted pine-trees clung on the bare rock allow us to see the far flash of the deep sea under a bright precipice of pine-needles or sometimes the attractive view of a golden small beach. Then, the charming suggestion of the landscape is sometimes interrupted by the ancient signs of man being now an essential element of the view: the proud Tower of Monte Pucci, an ancient rampart against the Saracens, near Peschici, and down, almost on the waves, a series of interlacing beams and nets, the so-called "trabucco", a very ancient fishing-tool, dating back to Phoenicians time, according to tradition.

Nevertheless, nature prevails again: from the beach of Calenella, at the bottom of a precipice almost hidden by the pine leaves, the coast again winds eastwards, interrupted by a series of small bays and glades as far as Vieste and the huge monolith called Pizzomunno. On the top of a rocky headland the medieval village stands out on the sea with its alleys and steps among the bright white houses; on the top, near to the Castle and Seggio, seat of the old municipality, the Basilica, one of the most ancient examples of Apulian architecture of the 11th century, though changed in the 18th century; in the inside the wooden statue of St. Mary of Merino in Quattrocento style and worshipped by all the local believers.

The village represents the fixed starting-point to explore the sea rocky gorges for which Gargano is famous: very beautiful are the Cave of Major Arch, the Cave of Snake, the Emerald Cave, that of Smugglers, the Great Sfondata, forty metres high and the Two Eyes, from whose opening the reflection of the sun in the sea flashes in an extraordinary play of shades.

From this heavenly place the panoramic road runs among bushes of rosemary, juniper and Aleppo pine-trees showing, at every bend, precipices, ravines, cliffs, rocks, unexpected small coves in the shadow of olive-trees and, before reaching Mattinata, it crosses the bridle-path which allows people to go up Mount Saraceno, the ancient headquarters of Muslims in Gargano, from which, according to a legend, Ettore Fieramosca was supposed to have thrown himself into the sea and southwards, it leads to Sacred Mount and the majestic remains of the Abbey of the Trinity.

The landscape of beech-woods, stone quarries and small coves almost suddenly changes, when we begin going down towards the Sipontine marshes: a series of different environment, from bogs to flooded meadows, an ideal habitat for many kinds of water fowls.

The exploration of this liquid universe can begin from Manfredonia, built in the middle of the 13th century by the Swabian Manfred, after that an earthquake had razed the nearby Siponto. For its position out of the marshy areas and for the remarkable depths of the gulf, the town, since the beginning of 15th century, has been considered one of the main ports of Northern Apulia; this situation brought about sieges, assaults and incursions: in 1528 there were the French led by Lautrech and in 1620 the conquest and the sack by the Turks.

Among the ruins of war and earthquakes, particularly baneful the ones in 1627 and 1646, monumental structures of great interest have survived such as: the Cathedral, raised by the archbishop Vincenzo Maria Orsini on the ruins of the ancient one destroyed by Ottoman troops, and the church of St. Domenico which in its front includes the original ogival porch of the Chapel of Maddalena, ordered to be built by the Charles II d'Angiò.

The Castle, begun by Manfred and completed by the Angevins, is composed of a four-sided donjon and four angular towers included in the building walls of the 15th century; recently restored, it is the seat of the National Archaeological Museum of Gargano where together with other prehistoric finds coming from "Coppa Nevigata" and from "Mount Saraceno", there are also many patterns of "stele daunie", unique stone documents.

Outside Manfredonia, along the road for Foggia, we find the Basilica of St. Mary the Greater, one of the most important Romanesque-Eastern buildings in Apulia, dating back to the first decades of 11th century and, near there, the ancient seat of the Teutonic Order

Trabucco (a very ancient fishing-tool) in Peschici

in Capitanata, the church of St. Leonardo of Siponto, embellished with a precious sculptured portal.

A wide and suggestive wet area extends along the boundaries of the town; this universe of archaic splendour begins on the left bank of the Candelaro river with the "Frattarolo Natural Preserve", 275 hectares wide: quagmires studded with bushes of tamarisks and reeds, run by herds of buffaloes where, in spring, small herons and other kinds of herons and stilt plovers stop; in winter, instead, in shallow water, ducks and small woodcocks nest, while the calls of curlews and lapwings echo in the air. On the other bank of the river, the "Daunia Risi", a preserve established in 1960, including 496 hectares of valleys of hunting and fishing and 1300 hectares of fields cultivated with cereals. Here we also find boundless extents of reed thickets, interrupted by ponds which, in cold months, host thousands of coots and ducks and in the hot ones, the "basettino" and the major "svasso"(other kind of birds).

If these wet areas in the South of Gargano represent the greatest places for those who love the mar-

Santa Maria Maggiore in Siponto

shes, the same is for the view of the coastal lakes of the North, separated by the relief of Mount Elio, once seat of the ancient "Devia" and by Sannicandro Garganico, a village of mysterious origins, being characteristic for the ancient village overlooked by the Cathedral and the Castle in Quattrocento style of Della Marra family.

Around Lesina the natural sight is fascinating: enormous grasslands, huge cornfields, old farmhouses in a proud loneliness and, on the horizon, the quiet expanse of the lake from which the Abbey of St. Mary of Ripalta stands out on a modest height. At a short distance, the preserve of Isle Wood keeps its own wild beauty intact: an unmetalled road crosses it

as far as Scampamorte Tower which appears, alone, on the wonderful sea of Gargano, a paradise for fishermen and archaeologists.

Its still unspoilt waters keep cernie (groupers), dentexes, saraghi (white breams), "corvine", octopuses, oysters, razor-clams, anchor-rings, cuttle-fishes, but these are not the only surprises being reserved for visitors. As a matter of fact, this whole part of the sea, now attended only by tourists, once was ploughed by the ships of Carthaginians, Romans, Saracen corsairs and warlike monks of Military Orders, Normans, Swabians, Angevins… towards Tremiti. We can easily suppose that something has remained of shipwrecks and skirmishes in the depths: in the beach of sea-gulls,

The lake of Lesina

for example, marble balls of different sizes, surely projectiles of culverins or catapults have been found together with amphorae, stone and bronze anchors, remains of hulls. But the real jewel of the Sea of Gargan is the Archipelago of Tremiti where there are all the natural beauties of the Headland: reefs, Cyclopean rocks, small quiet coves, steep cliffs, mysterious caves alternate.

San Domino, the greater isle, is thickly covered with expanses of Aleppo pine-trees; interesting even the natural hollows: from the Cave of Salt to that of Violets; from the Cave of Flying-gurnards to that of Sea Ox, the latter being overlooked by Appicco and Ripa of Falcons, two very high rocks whose faces fall sheer to the sea where the hawk of the queen, the peregrine hawk, the pale swift nest. The second isle of the archipelago of Tremiti, San Nicola, has always played an important role and now it represents the historical, administrative and religious centre of the whole archipelago: Augustus is supposed to have

abandoned the nephew Giulia here till her death and Charlemagne to have exiled Paolo Diacono. Here the Abbey of St. Mary to the Sea (Santa Maria al Mare) was founded by a hermit led by the apparitions of the Virgin to a fabulous treasure by means of which he built a temple in the place of the miraculous finding.

The documentary history of the Archipelago begins when the Benedictines of Montecassino arrived here: they built the factories on the North side together with the church; in the 15th century these buildings were restored by Lateran canons and widened adding new architectural elements, besides, the defensive structures were also reinforced beginning from the resort itself where today there is a slope leading to the inside. On the contrary, the Convent must have been provided with a cylindrical donjon and high crenellated walls only since the 14th century to which the external wall and the moat were successively added.

The economic-military power of St. Mary to the Sea, during the 16th century, was so much that it was

Tremiti Islands

able to hold out bravely against the assault of Solimano II in 1567; but, after that, its fortune began declining till 1782, when Ferdinando IV of Borboun abolished the Abbey later transformed into a prison, a sad function ended after Fascism's fall.

The last of the major isles is La Caprara, once woody and rich in capers from which its name originates, it is the symbol of loneliness with its flat and bony aspect. In the middle of the archipelago we find the Rock of Cretaccio, in the shape of half-moon and the black and wrinkled rock of La Vecchia (The Old Woman): both of them desert, are populated by night, according to a popular superstition; the first is haunted by the ghost of a prisoner who was executed there, the second one by an old woman being intent on spinning wool between sky and sea.

Tavoliere

At the foot of Gargano, between the Apennines and the sea, the Daunia plain stretches majestically, seat of very ancient cultures from time immemorial, whose remarkable charm is today witnessed by the most famous neolithic spot: Passo di Corvo (the Pass of the Crow), brought to light by recent excavations near Foggia. During the year Tavoliere shows itself to the visitor as dressed in iridescent colours: it is golden in summer, green and scented when the rest of Italy is

The Pass of the Crow

still under the winter frost, red for the burning stubbles on July nights.

San Severo, the capital of wine, inhabited from remote times, as proved by the remains of prehistoric, Dauni and Roman settlements stands out as a guard of its Western entry, in the middle of various roads coming from Gargano and Subapennines. The legend makes its origin date back to the Diomedic "Castel Drion" that is "Village of oak-trees"; as a matter of fact "Fanum Sancti Severi" was a suburb from Longobard origins, around which developed the village which, being given from Guiscardo to the Benedictines of Torremaggiore, got freedom in 1116 thanks to "Charta Libertatis" of the abbot Adenulfo. Episcopal seat and feud of the illustrious Di Sangro family, it preserves traces of its own famous past in the monuments surviving from the violent earthquake of 1627: the church of St. Mary, already existing in 12th century and raised as cathedral in 1580, and the thirteenth-century churches of St. Severino the Abbot with clear Romanesque features on the front, of St. Nicola, inside embellished with a valuable wooden choir and four great statues by the Venetian Ambrogio Piazza, and of St John the Baptist, important for the paintings by Nicola Mensele. In Baroque style, on the contrary, the church of St. Lorenzo, the Sanctuary of Madonna of Soccorso (Aid) and the Celestines Palace.

From San Severo Tavoliere stretches southwards

Cerignola, the bell tower of the Cathedral

On previous page: the archaeological area of Herdonia

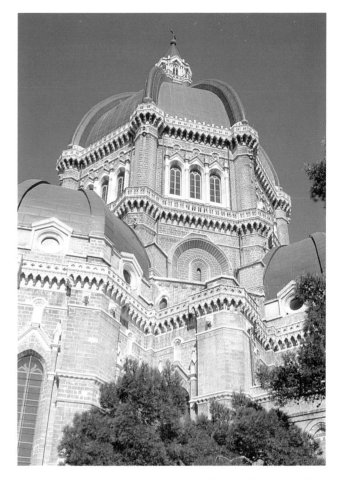

showing a suggestive landscape sometimes interrupted by testimonies of archaic presence such as the ancient Herdonea, in Ordona, whose classical and medieval traces, destroyed by the Carthaginian Annibal and by the Byzantine Emperor Costante, have been brought to light by the Belgian Archaeological Mission led by Professor Jean Mertens: rectangular building walls, being 730 metres long and 300 wide and suddenly out of it an elliptical Roman Amphitheatre perhaps dating back to the 18th century BC.

At a short distance from each other, the small Communes of Ortanuova, Stornara, Stornarella and Carapelle, once the "Royal Seats", characterize Tavoliere as far as Cerignola, heir to the powerful Geryon, often mentioned by Pliny and Plutarch, and where we must visit the Cathedral with dome and ribs similar to the ones of St. Maria del Fiore by Brunelleschi, built by the architect Giuseppe Pisanti for the benefactor Paolo Tonti's wish at the end of 19th century; and the Plain of hollows, a wide square full of calcareous cippi, marks of wide underground silos, authentic warehouses being from two to three metres deep and able to keep 1600 hectolitres of corn at most.

This landscape of cornfields and wide vineyards planted around Cerignola by the French family De La Rochefoucault and by Pignatelli family suddenly interrupts in the South and it offers such an odd loneliness that every kind of human presence seems to be disappeared: the salt pans of Margherita of Savoia, extending for about four thousand hectares between Zapponeta and the homonymous resort. Here the natural sight is composed of a geometrical series which always repeats as far as the horizon: tens of basins of brown and reddish waters crossed by thin embankments of beaten ground. About three thousand water fowls occupy this immense and famous wet area: in winter ducks and waders; in spring, instead, in the low vegetation, the so called "avocet-ta", the stilt bird of Italy and the "fraticello" nest. The place which offers a safe refuge to such precious fauna is also famous for the remarkable therapeutical qualities of its waters, thanks to which the Spa of Margherita of Savoia, now widened and renovated, has become famous in the whole Peninsula.

In the middle of Tavoliere, not so far from the mythical Arpi, rises Foggia, from which it is possible, in short time, to reach every place of the Province, even the farthest one such as: Tremiti Islands thanks to the fast run of helicopters which provide the daily connection.

The town, from Norman origins, is one thousand

Foggia, the Customs Palace

years old, but it is almost new for the most part because at first it was completely destroyed by an earthquake in 1731, then by the bombardments of the last conflict: we can trace its ancient memories only in the three major town cultural institutions such as: the Record Office, the Civic Museum and the Provincial Library.

Therefore the traces of the past splendour of Foggia are scarce: the Romanesque Cathedral, wished by Guglielmo the Good, whose inside is rich in precious works of art among which there is the oil painting representing the apostle Peter by Giuseppe Ribera, the great fan-light by Francesco De Mura reproducing the Multiplication of loaves and the Crucified by Pietro Frasa; the precious Crypt, with the four magnificent capitals by Nicola di Bartolomeo; and, near there, the porch of the protomaster Bartolomeo from Foggia, built in a wall with a stone inscription: «Hoc fieri iussit Fredericus Caesar...». Under this arch, seven centuries ago there was the alternation of the guests invited by the Swabian Emperor to visit the royal palace extolled by contemporary chroniclers for the wonderful beauty of fountains, gardens and statues. But nothing has remained: only the nostalgia for a myth survives.

Here and there among palaces and streets of an ordinary town, there are the Baroque signs (for the most part) of the recent history: the churches of Our Lady of Sorrows, of St. John, St. Agostino, of Purgatory, of St. Domenico and the austere Customs Palace, the latter being linked to the reminiscences of "Mena delle pecore" (Sheep trade) which, regulated in 1447 by Alfonso from Aragon, lasted till Borbouns' time and transformed the lands of Tavoliere in a bleak and barren moor which only in the months of November and May became livelier but soon after it came back to its usual condition of silence and desolation.

During this very long time, in Foggia, the local economy was in the hands of few people such as: the noble Neapolitans, the great indifferent feudatories, the rich breeders from Abruzzi, responsible for taking away two thirds of the plain from agriculture.

In the shadow of this economic-political power, interrupted by short popular experiences such as: the rebellion of Sabato Pastore in 1648 and the Parthenopean Republic, there was the growth of a weak and subjected middle class of craftsmen and merchants, lawyers and civil servants, all of them immigrating into the town only during the period of winter pastures. As a consequence of such socio-economical conditions, there was the development, outside the town centre, of a ward of isolated and poor shepherds: the "terrazzani" (terrace-dwellers), who being survived till some decade ago, have shown a typical social phenomenon of Foggia. They dwelled around the church of Crosses, outside the town perimeter, and there they created an original popular suburb, whose long rows of buildings without any windows, with an entry on the top with some steps raised to the roadway, are surely one of few existing examples of poor urban architecture.

The same misery must have characterized the other wards of post-earthquake Foggia till the first half of the 19th century when the new noble landowners, created by French Decade and become rich after the liquidation of State pastures, began refining the urban scenery through their tasteful houses, while, at the same time, the architect Luigi Oberty, sent from Naples, contributed to ennoble the aspect of the town, planning the Pronaos of the Town-Park, Ferdinando Theatre, today called Giordano, the Colonnade of church of St. Francesco Saverio.

In the last twenty years of the 19th century in Capitanata like in most other Southern provinces, the landowners' classes succeeded in controlling the local power and in the thirties of the 20th century, they themselves commissioned the engineer Cesare Albertini to plan such town changes that now it has lost its rustic characteristic and has shown the present modern character. During the phases of the evolution of the Fascist "Great Foggia", rose Podestà Palace and Studies' Palace; the Prefecture; the Army Barracks, today seat of a Police School; Maria Grazia Barone Charitable Organization; the Palace of the Aqueduct of Apulia; the structure of "Stallion Horses". The town changed its aspect definitively owing to the elimination of crumbling streets and decrepit 18th wards where sometimes precious monuments were not always rescued; finally there was a more modern street system: in the ex ward Scopari, now Dante street, the important financial centre was created; there was also the connection between the railway station and the new ward of the ancient part through Corso Vittorio Emanuele, overlooked by the Neoclassical Cavour Square where, unfortunately, it has remained little of the original architectural elegance.

Just outside the capital, which, after its post-war reconstruction, is living a tumultuous socio-urban expansion, the wide extent of cornfields triumphs again, whose sleepy quietness stops and becomes livelier on the occasion of local religious festivities about the worship of Mary, traditionally coinciding with the beginning and the end of different cultivations. So, in the area of Foggia, on the last Friday of April, the "Ride of Angels" inaugurates the annual opening of the Sanctuary of the Crowned Virgin, destination for pilgrimages from the whole Region and the neighbouring ones for forty days; in the South, in Cerignola, on 8th September, the believers go to the procession of Madonna of Ripalta carried in a sort of basin full of flowers and angels; in the North, instead, in San Severo, it is Madonna of Olive-grove who, among a

crowd of peasants, in procession is carried on a cart decorated with olive and oak branches. Particularly important, likewise interesting for historical references connected with them, are, finally, the worship for the Madonna of Seven Veils of Foggia celebrated on 22nd of March, in the anniversary of the earthquake of 1731; and the Madonna of Victory of Lucera reminding us of the triumph over the Saracens on 14th August, 1300.

After the short parenthesis of such rites, the bright and dazzling light which reflects its splendour on the undulating hills of Subapennines also overlooks again silent and undisputed today, like a thousand years ago, on the boundless plain.

The Dauno Subapennines

Clear, at the end of the road which from Foggia goes up along the foot of the plateau, stands out the pointed arch of the Angevin Gate of Roman and Saracen Lucera: within the walls there is an elegant small town and, in the middle of Classical ruins, well-lighted streets and houses of a disappeared nobility, there is the Gothic Cathedral ordered to be built by Charles d'Angiò.

Of the most ancient traces, except for the Amphitheatre, restored in 1932, today, no other important elements remain: the town centre, almost completely destroyed by Byzantines in 663, was sacked again and again successively in order to find building material. It rose again during the Middle Ages thanks to Frederick II who transferred there the Arab populations of Sicily, to put an end to their rebellions: the half-abandoned suburb, then, was enlivened by an intense building activity which placed the labyrinthical space of Islamic settlement on the rigid geometrical system of the Roman one.

On the Swabians' falling, the Saracen colony was destroyed and the subsequent Angevin building works, restoring the Roman street system, gave a more schematic aspect to the town which became, from the 16th century to the 18th one, a place of residence for many noble families who built there houses of great architectural elegance such as Scassa, Petrilli, Nicastri, Mozzagrugno palaces being these two last ones seats of "Giuseppe Fiorelli" Civic Museum and "Ruggero Bonghi" Library.

Meeting-point of different civilizations, Lucera preserves their most important traces in the Cathedral, built at the beginning of the 14th century in

Lucera, the Amphitheatre

the place where the great Saracen mosque rose; in the church of St. Domenico and in that of St. Francesco. But nothing of the imperial town nor of the Muslim isle situated in the heart of Christian Apulia has survived, yet no place represents the spirit and reminiscences of Frederick more than this and the majestic castle which, along the extreme edge of Lucera's plateau, shows its own walls in one kilometre perimeter between the two imposing donjons of the King and the Queen, and it will be always the castle of Frederick for anyone even if it was built by the Angevins on the ruins of the imperial palace.

Together with Lucera, Troia, the capital of Guelph party, situated on the opposite hill, has also come to an end: its history has ended when the Swabian completely destroyed it; since then it hasn't any longer revived even when the Papacy has triumphed over the temporal power of the Empire. Today it is a small village, but the superb bulk of the Romanesque Cathedral still overlooks proud and powerful on the houses, with its wonderful front, decorated with sculptures and architectural elements gravitating towards the rose window the stone symbol of the heroic town.

The front of the
Cathedral of Troia

Sant'Agata di Puglia

The inside of the Cathedral has three aisles supported by twelve marble columns and another one, near to the first on right as if it symbolised Christ with the apostles; the pulpit dates back to 1158, while the transept is the outcome of the construction of the two chapels of Patrons Saints and of Our Lady ,the Virgin Mary received into Heaven.

Their porctals were moulded by Oderisio from Benevento and the images of the bishops on their bronze panels, like those on the "Exultet"- the illuminated parchment documents of 11th-12th centuries preserved in the treasure of diocesan Museum -, still rela-

te today's events of this stronghold of freedom of citizens which was once famous in Italy.

In the north-west of Lucera, on the utmost slopes of the Apeninnes which, between the Fortore and the Ofanto rivers, go down in the shape of an amphitheatre, twenty-eight Communes are behind one another similar to natural sentries to watch the borders of Capitanata. They are from ten to twenty kilometres far from each other, they are sometimes separated by a distance of a thousand metres, among coppices and silent gorges. All around: either higher, or lower mountains follow one another till they fade away in

the distance and between a height and another one, valleys, small streams and, everywhere, as far as the eye can reach, big and small woods sometimes from poetic names: Wood of Protection, of Crib, of St. Cristoforo, Pine-wood of Madonnina and the authentic strip of Hearthly Paradise that is the Garden of Sulphur, between Biccari and Roseto, where, in the middle of a luxuriant vegetation and natural springs gushing from mountain to valley, lies the lake of Peschiera.

People who pass these districts can't help being charmed by their changing views: very loose rivers and streams; towers, castles and churches; cornfields, vineyards and olive-groves. Here the land is dry and stony, humpy or sheer, barren and avaricious; but, at any depth, the peasant is always able to make it fruitful, practising that intensive cultivation which is imposed by nature. But this is also the place made mythical and sacred by woods, rocks and religious rites of population: inhabitants from Volturino in September, offer a scene of biblical flavour, during the rural procession of Madonna of Serritella, when the crowd as thick as a herd climbs along steep short ways, in search of the Protectress; or population from Motta who, in May, leaves houses and shops and the Sanctuary of Mount Sambuco in order to implore mercy to the patron St. John.

In the Subapennines we can meet the descendants

and sometimes mysterious events of this part of Capitanata.

After passing Lucera's fortress, if we go towards Campobasso, suddenly we will meet the imposing bulk of Chair of the Devil, the impressive ruin of the disappeared Montecorvino which, being destroyed many times by the Normans and Angevins, was abandoned after the earthquake of 1456. Nevertheless, its inhabitants did not abandon the area and created two new villages: Motta Montecorvino and Pietra Montecorvino. The former had donjons and town walls in the 15th century where five gates opened, three of which still exist; the latter, instead, makes us relive the mysterious and a little dark atmosphere of the Middle Ages in its intact old part, in the middle of which rises the ducal palace, dominated by a forty-metre high tower and the 18th-century Mother Church, dominated by the imposing portico and by the artistic major gate.

From Pietra, covering only about thirty kilometres, we can reach Volturara Appula, where the fortified residence of Caracciolo family still stands; San Marco la Catola, proud of its 15th-century Castle, and Celenza Valfortore, an ancient feud of Gambacorta Marquises, from whose 16th-century fortress defended by a crenellated cylindrical donjon, we can overlook the surrounding landscape completely as far as the dam of Occhito, one of the widest artificial lakes in Europe, extending for thirteen square kilometres, sixty metres deep and 333 million cubic metres wide.

At a short distance it is worth visiting Roseto, characteristic for the baronial tower and the lanes adorned with noble palaces; the Arab Tertiveri, seat of a 16th-century feudal palace and Biccari defended by a cylindrical Byzantine tower. Little far from it, there is Dragonara: on a terrace which appears on Fortore,

of ancient foreign colonies whose memories relieve today in the exotic charm of the dialect: Celle and Faeto, where, in the 14th century, Charles I d'Angiò created Provençal communities and finally Casalnuovo in whose language the accent of the Slavonians of the Albanian coast who, expelled by the Turks, settled here in the 16th century, relives.

But this is also the land of the castles and towers which, in spite of the present isolation, keep watching over those same countries and woods which, in the past, they dominated proudly, when they were the residence of illustrious families of the Kingdom. Following this itinerary means plunging into exciting

Bovino, the Castle

natural border between Apulia and Molise, rises its quadrangular castle, defined by a tower on each side, two round and two square ones.

The strategic importance of the place caused, in the past, the successive fortification of original Byzantine construction at first by the Swabians and then by the Aragoneses. Dragonara, therefore, together with Troia, Fiorentino and Civitate, about the year one thousand, represented the extreme defence of Capitanata against the Longobard princedom of Benevento: of such ancient fortifications only the Castle of Dragonara, the ruins of Fiorentino, recently brought to light, and the ones of Civitate have survived.

Coming back to Foggia, we will reach Bovino, nestled among the gorges which were dens of legendary brigands, hidden to those who run across the valley, protected by winds and men. Today of the ancient fame only the sacred myth of the Sanctuary of Valleverde survives, whose new construction was inaugurated by the Pope Giovanni Paolo II, during his visit to Capitanata in 1987. Instead, nothing of the ancient proud power exists: Bovino, like Troia and

Bovino, the Castle

Lucera is also a mountain village bearing the signs of an illustrious past such as: the low and dark 12th-century Cathedral, a precious example in Romanesque style with previous Byzantine elements and Gothic superimpositions. The castle, still watches over the whole village threatening in its unchanged and strong structure; it was built by the Norman Drogone, count of Apulia, on the ruins of a Roman fortress, widened by Frederick II and successively changed and it was transformed into the residence of dukes of Guevara in 17th century.

With Bovino and its mountains, with the clayey hills of the Apennines, on which there are Ascoli Satriano, proud of the ducal palace of Marulli, Deliceto, surrounding the imposing thirty-metre high donjon, placed side by side by two towers, Candela, Accadia and from which appear the white houses of Sant'Agata, overlooked by the Norman-Swabian Castle, we are already outside the province of Foggia, towards Basilicata, towards Irpinia: in the same way, in the north, Abruzzi open behind the trees and the green pastures of Val Fortore.

Trani

The province of Bari

Bisceglie, the dolmen

The land of Bari, to be better understood and loved, must be visited with calm and quietness, in order to read again the social and economic history in the artistic, sculptural and pictorial manifestations. A history which becomes clear above all when we search into the reasons of commissioned works, both from noble classes and popular ones, or of the origins of the leading political parties in the different phases of the history of this land. It has always been such a meeting-point for worlds and cultures that it has appeared subjected to the rulers who have alternated but, at the same time, it shows to a more careful eye, the ability to elaborate the essential features to get an autonomous and characterizing synthesis.

If it is famous for the lack of water, for erosive cracks (swamps and ravines) which date back to prehistoric age, it is also famous for the traces of past civilizations. From the dolmens of Bisceglie to Peuceti (in the first millenium BC.) till the partecipation in the worlds of Magna Graecia and Rome which mainly happened along the Traian and Appian Ways, passing through that double row of settlements placed along the Adriatic coast and, in parallel, in the inside at about 10-15 kilometres.

The memories of Byzantine and Norman-Swabian revival still survive, in the stones of buildings and in

The Swabian Castle in Trani

the memories of documents, in this area of frequent commercial exchanges with the Muslim East and the Holy Land. A Romanesque art which mediates and synthesizes in itself originally the influences of the most advanced culture of the centre of Europe moderated by the Mediterranean character which our population has never lost. The castles, the towers, the bastions and the great number of big and small churches and cathedrals, all of them rich and jealous of their own autonomy and acquired privileges bear witness to this situation.

An expansion which goes on, in an atmosphere of reletive autonomy for the Communes of Apulia, till the whole 16th century having cultural and commercial relations with the other Adriatic shore and the nearby East, for the strong influence of Venice, too; a life, during the Renaissance, which we can notice in a great number of refined palaces scattered in the unknown old parts of our towns.

There is a more general crisis in the 17th century when the already strong feudal pressure weighs upon the Communities (Universities) which are in debt and abandoned by a careless central power in trouble (vicereign of Spain). Some renewal, between the 18th and 19th centuries, allows Apulia to overcome the building and customs barriers, giving way to another

period of life in Apulia which is known very little from the historical-artistical point of view when the expansion of towns, the constitution of their new villages of Napoleonic and Neobourbon period, have been often victims of unitary historiography which hasn't acknowledged the attempt to organize the State again in the pre-unitary Reign.

Though in a less emphasised way, the transformation of ancient villages has often gone on with the demolition and opening of streets, at least till the Great War. Contemporarily the definitive arrangement of cemeterial structures takes place in the towns where we can admire the most successful examples of

that sequence of "styles", from the Neogothic to modern ones, which followed one another between two centuries.

The provincial itinerary doesn't begin from the capital, as we could suppose, but from Canosa lying almost on the Ofanto which separates, in the north, the Land of Bari and Capitanata to go on with the ideal descent of "foreign" visitor which slowly gets used to our world, to our landscape.

Canosa has always been an important road junction because it is at the crossroads between the Traian Way and a branch of the Appian way which led to the Adriatic sea, passing for Venusia.

It is a place of important archaeological discoveries witnessed by great and rich funeral hypogea, by the remains of the amphitheatre, of the spas and the bridge on the Ofanto (during the second century AD.) whose materials were used by the bishop Sabino(514-566), the creator of the transformation of the town realized in order to gather the population around the Christian basilicas. In the town, therefore, rise a lot of worship buildings: a Cathedral (St. Mary) and a baptistery (St. John the Baptist and St. Salvatore), as well as a basilica with a sepulchral part in it.

The medieval period (11th century) bears witness to the widening of the old cathedral, recently devoted to St. John and Paul, with the most up-to-date craftsmen of Romanesque age which establish a Latin cross plan covered with five domes. Now in the building which appears on Vittorio Veneto square, in particular we can admire the bishop's chair made by Romualdo (a throne on elephantins) and the pulpit with the eagle bearing a lectern, made by Acceptus. From the right-side transept we can reach the funeral mausoleum with a square plan surmounted by a small dome by Boemondo from Antiochia closed by a rich bronze door decorated with elements of eastern inspiration representing animals . St. John's baptistery in Matteotti street is, though in the rich panorama of Palaeochristian buildings of Canosa, a twelve side

Canosa, the remains of the basilica o St. Leucio

architectural jewel on a Greek cross plan with a font in the middle of it.

Canosa is the seat of a Civic Museum where there are a lot of stone pieces with inscriptions, sculptures, bas-reliefs, pieces of sarcophagi and precious collections of pottery from Canosa, found during the town excavations; and there are also small bronze pieces, glasses, coins and jewels.

We can easily notice geometrical floor mosaics with images of plants and animals among the remains of the basilica of St. Leucio, outside the town, dating back to the bishop Sabino's time, and in the same way, the historical stratification between the Italic time and the consequent early Middle Ages' widening.

On the road which from Canosa leads to Barletta, where in 216 BC. Hannibal defeated the Romans, there is Canne della Battaglia; here it is possible to see the archaeological area and the relative Antiquarium.

The present Barletta preserves its most ancient part in the "civita", with a fish-bone shaped plan with the central axis touching the Cathedral, and parallel to the sea, full of narrow blocks of houses. The 11th-13th centuries, more than the mythical foundation by the count Pietro in 1050, bear witness to the construction of the town with the contemporary development of the suburb of St. Giacomo, place of settlement for immigrants from Canne. It is between these two villages that the great church of the Holy Sepulchre has existed since the 12th century, in Gothic-Burgundian shapes, built by the monks of the homonymous Order coming from the Holy Land, where the cross-shaped pillars support the cross-vaults, further construction belonging to the 15th-century; a hospital of Pilgrims is annexed to this structure. On the side of the same church there is the famous Giant of Barletta, a late Roman bronze sculpture, about five metres high and representing an emperor.

Suddenly the town developed very quickly not only thanks to the wealth of local feudality, but also to the considerable circulation of capitals linked to the intense religious movement which bore witness to the transfer of the seat of the archdiocese of Nazareth from Palestine to the church of St. Mary "extra moenia" (outside the walls) at the beginning of the 14th century.

On the eastern side, the Norman-Swabian Castle separates and defends the town from the sea; it was widened, in a project also planning the reconstruction of the town-walls and the town, by the Angevins and, successively, by the Spaniards in the 16th century. Through this last plan, the three suburbs of St. Giacomo, Sette Rue and the "civita" are about forty hectares wide and they host almost 20.000 inhabitants. In the recently restored castle, there are the Civic

Canne della Battaglia

Museum and De Nittis Picture Gallery with the homonymous collection given to the town; we can also admire the paintings of Neapolitan school of famous painters such as: Luca Giordano and Francesco Solimena as well as various archaeological pieces among which stands out the stone bust of Frederick II.

But it is the Renaissance which marks an enrichment of the town due to outstanding buildings of singular beauty included in a simpler context. Corso Garibaldi, beginning from the apse of the church of the Holy Sepulchre, shows Gentile-Baldacchini palace (14th century) on left and the church of St. Domenico on right. If we go on, after passing the imposing Bonelli palace (14th century) with its big colonnade on the ground floor, finally we will reach the Medieval Cathedral, successively widened from the side of the apse through shapes reminding us of Gothic style. The high bell tower, placed on the left side of the building, still keeps the original possibility to walk under it.

We must also visit the nearby church of St. Andrea where there are a 17th-century wooden choir and a Madonna with the Infant Jesus by Alvise Vivarini together with the sepulchral monument of Fraggianni family. In Cialdini street, among other important religious buildings and the monument to 13 people of the challenge stands out the splendid

palace of Marra, recently under repair, a magnificent Renaissance residence which, besides its rich portal, shows an interesting and charming portico on the side of the sea. On the opposite side of the town, in Corso Vittorio Emanuele, there is the 18th-century Curci Theatre, a real jewel, restored in the last years.

If we go on along the coast we will meet Trani, which we can identify with the Turenum of the Imperial Age's Tabula Peutingeriana, but late news about the present town can be found in the quotation of a via antiqua (1035) where the first buildings would probably be built. Instead, the town was systematized by Frederick II with the building of the second town-walls and the quadrangular-shaped castle built by the imperial architect Philip Chinard which still today preserves the original constructive austerity even if it shows the subsequent restoration works (1310 ca) by the French architect Pierre of Angicourt to whom the great spur towards the town and the colonnade below are attributed. The discoveries, happened during the recently ended campaign of restoration, are very interesting.

The town, since its first origin a reference-point for great trade, boasts the most ancient Medieval maritime statutes (1063) and it comprehends different quarters referring to the immigrants (coming from Venice, Pisa, Amalfi, and Jewish people, etc.); between the 15th and 16th centuries it was given as a feud together with other strategic ports of the Region, to the Serenissima (as Venice was celled).

In spite of its commercial crisis linked to the general one of the Reign, at the end of the 16th century the Royal Court was founded giving greater cultural importance to the town till it became the capital of Land of Bari and its episcopal seat became archbishop's Metropolia including the nearby seats of Barletta, Bisceglie, Salpi, Nazareth, Monteverde, etc.

The image of essential unity that can be noticed in the ancient suburb, if we go along Beltrami street, depends on the group of many luxury palaces which

separated by twenty-four twin columns. We must visit the crypt below, devoted to the Saint where a thick group of columns supports a series of refined capitals.

Going towards the port and along the shore, at first we will meet Caccetta palace (1450 ca) and then, set in the homogeneous building area, the apsidal part of the church of All Saints where stands out the great central window enriched with two decorative concentric bands with griffins and lions bearing columns on them.

On the coast the church of St. Mary of Martyrs, founded by the Norman William I (1162) in the place of a cemetery of the crusaiders warriors and near the pre-existing Hospital of Cruisaders shows us that we are approaching Molfetta.

The original suburb has an elliptical form with herring-bone streets and it is situated on the coastal protrusion of St. Andrea, whose existence is already witnessed with the name of Melphi about the 10th century. It is a town which develops especially in that period with its population probably coming from the famous Pulo (a natural dolina, thirty-five metres deep).

Its seafaring activity and municipal freedom are already proved by the commercial pact with the Dalmatian community of Dubrovnik, as it is an active centre of agrarian production and a market attended by Venetians as well as Dalmatians, etc. In the 16th century even if it was completely subjected to feudalism, the construction of town-walls was planned and, though never completed, comprehended the houses of common people while nobles and patricians preferred renewing the factories of the old suburb. During the following centuries this tendency changed so much that, at the end of the 18th century, it caused the transfer of the relics of St. Corrado from the Cathedral to the present Cathedral.

The former (dating back to the half of 12th century), opposite to the sea, faces with the ex-palace and episcopal seminary (which has a beautiful double balcony) a bare bench leading to the port.

would be worth mentioning. At the end of the street the sight is remarkable, from the square before it, stands out the Cathedral including the Castle, the law Courts and the palace of the Archives.

The Cathedral really comprehends stratified sacred buildings, built in different times in order to satisfy the changed and greater requirements of worship. The church of St. Mary was already built on a previous plan (5th-7th centuries), but the new and imposing building (1159-86) devoted to St. Nicola Pellegrino, has the plan of a basilica with three aisles

Trani, the front of the Cathedral

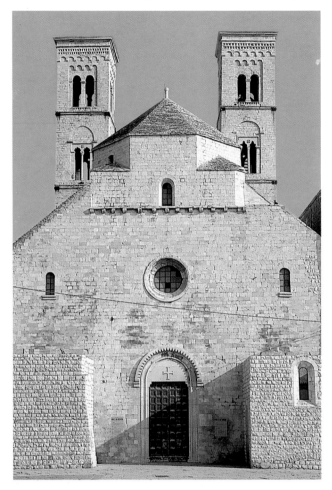

The building, completed only at the end of the 13th century, for the clear difficulty to solve the technical theme of a great church with three lined domes, has the plan of a basilica with contracted transepts and a double feature, a bell tower united in the construction with the apsidal part which, on the contrary, appears flat.

Entering the ancient suburb and going along St. Orsola street, we will see many heraldic insignia which bear witness to the presence of patrician palaces of the 16th and 17th centuries. At the end of the street we will be, in the square, in front of the town-hall, once the House of Templari dinasty to which a homonymous Hall probably dating back to the 12th century is annexed; near there on the right, in the suburb, we can visit the 18th-century church of St. Peter with a beautiful front and a Baroque bell tower; in the inside we can find the paintings by Nicola Porta, apprentice of the most famous painter from Molfetta: Corrado Giaquinto (1703-65).

On the border between the village of St. Andrea and the following ones, we find the Cathedral of the Virgin Mary received into Heaven which has got in its Baroque inside a series of important works by C. Rosa, N. Porta and C. Giaquinto.On one side there is the town Park behind which we can admire the Calvary planned by the architect De Judicibus in the 19th century.

After Molfetta, going into the inside and passing over Terlizzi, we will reach Ruvo located on the first smooth "step" of Murgia among endless vineyards and oliveyards. The ancient Rubi, already on the Traiana Way, keeps an interesting collection of tropical local pots (5th-3rd centuries BC.) in the Jatta museum together with other finds which bear witness to the relations of the town with the other cultures of the opposite Adriatic shore.

The quadrangular shape in which the ancient part of the town is included probably proves the influence of Roman foundation defined by four wide main streets. Starting from Bovio square, in one of the corners, we suddenly find the neo-Classical palace Jatta, seat of the above-mentioned museum. From the same square, taking Rosario street towards the inside, we can see the two Renaissance donjons which show a fairly complete part of the Aragonese wall.

In Queen Margherita square, on the contrary, there is the town hall (already Avitaia) in a 16th-century building, with the chapel of St. Rocco on its side. In the same place appears the church of the Redeemer, realized using some remaining rooms of the Medieval palace Melodia, already baronial seat. Taking Vuccolo street

Molfetta, the Cathedral

now, we reach in front of the church of Purgatory, built for a greater devotion to the cave below of St. Cleto, mythical bishop of the town during the year 44.

But the most important monument of the town is without any doubt the Cathedral with the characteristic front with very sloping side-pitches which give the image of magnificence and rush towards the top. The church, generally supposed to date back to the period between 11th and 13th centuries, has recently been object of careful restorations which have emphasised the continuity of worship in comparison with a previous building with a three-apse crypt and also, below, pieces of floor-mosaics dating back to the Palaeochristian age and some cisterns.

From Ruvo we can directly reach Castel del Monte, Frederick II's hunting residence, built about 1240, placed on a height which overlooks a wide area. It is the stone transposition of the most cultural conception of time, for someone it goes further and refers to cosmic conceptions with dark and forewarning meanings.

Castel del Monte was used for different but not always right and suitable purposes, in spite of its beauty and prestige, now it finds itself far from being the capital of the Reign. We can see the restoration works concerning a lot of the external masonry being worn away by time and the despoiling of the internal one, once being defended by precious marbles previously removed.

Coming back to Ruvo and going on towards Bari, we will find, in the middle of a wide land cultivated with olives, Bitonto, which rose, at the beginning, around the small church of St. Peter, already a pagan worship place devoted to the goddess Minerva as some coins bearing the wording: "Bytontynon" would indirectly bear witness to it.

The inner dynamic of the town, from the Roman Age to the Middle Ages, has favoured the central part of the town or the settlement scattered in the hamlets of the surrounding countryside. The turning point occured in Norman Age, on the initiative of the bishop Arnolfo, when the organization in parishes in the inside corresponded to the well-arranged walls.

But the fundamental event for the town is surely the building of the Cathedral (at the beginning of the 12th century) which, for its rhythm and stylishness, is the most beautiful one in the South of Italy. The tri-partite front keeps and blends a series of elements which emphasise the wish to represent the natural and supernatural things together in the stone. The southern side emphasises the close relation between the blind arcades and the overhanging mullioned windows with six lights with small columns and engraved capitals. Nowadays closed because it is under repair, under its floor it has revealed a series of structures and a very beautiful mosaic representing a gryphon.

The wide area and the production of oils have made the town, since the Angevin Age, such an important commercial and cultural centre that, after a period in which it had become a feud (1318-1553), it was redeemed through the payment of 60.000 ducats and above all thanks to the Spanish middle class and the bishop Cornelio Musso. It is the beginning of a new phase of reconstruction of the town through the restoration of many ancient sacred buildings in which the painter Carlo Rosa and his apprentices are often involved.

But the heart of the historical town is worth visiting, where every corner stirs up a new emotion, in Cavour square stands out the church with only a nave, devoted to St. Gaetano with a wooden ceiling painted by Carlo Rosa, but we are attracted by the loggia in Cinquecento style of Sylos-Calò palace which shows on its front, in Rogadeo street, the great porch leading to the inside court-yard enriched with a colonnade.

If we go on and leave the church of Purgatory which we can easily identify for the sinister sculptures of skeletons and repentant souls on its front, we will arrive at Bove palace in Seicento style where the loggia enriches the portal leading to the courtyard and roof-garden. The passage under another arch makes us approach Rogadeo palace, now seat of the Library and Civic Museum keeping an interesting collection of Apulian painters during the 19th century, besides the archaeological material of the place.

If we turn right, suddenly we will find ourselves in front of the southern side of the cathedral whose external part has already been described; in the inside, on the contrary, it shows a typical shape of a basilica but with forms and proportions being out of ordinary. The present image is the result of hard works of restoration happened at the end of the last century, many

Ruvo, the front of the Cathedral and
details

Castel del Monte

Bitonto, the colonnade of the Cathedral

elements are fragmentary or have been restored, while the precious ambo, made by a certain Nicolaus was placed again on the angular pillar.

Taking the way again we had better observe the other side of Franco-Spinelli palace, enriched with a series of Andalusian wrought-iron balconies and a porch decorated with Renaissance bass-reliefs probably dating back to influences from Dalmatia and Veneto. At the end of St. Francesco street there is the homonymous late 13th-century church of which only the front remains, while on right side, there is the small and half-remote church of St. Peter in castro, a primitive settlement of the town.

Arriving at Bari from the hinterland, rather than from the sea, means passing through a large industrial area which precedes wide suburbs before reaching the old part of the town.

The strategic position, on a protrusion of the Adriatic, has always made it a place of primary political and economical importance. The finds, dating back to the Bronze Age, bear witness to the constant attendances of the place which, during the Roman Age, becomes a municipium. The ups and downs of the conflicts between the Longobards and the Byzantines also cause, during a short period, the establishment of an emirate on the part of the Mussulmans (847-71) and then the conquest of the Byzantines again for almost a century till, in 1071, the Norman Roberto il Guiscardo conquered it definitively.

This is the period in which (1087) enterprising sailormen from Bari stole the relics of St. Nicola from Mira, later preserved in the homonymous basilica which has been compared to a beautiful stone jewelcase, beginning to be built two years later. A reference point in its style for the contemporary buildings of the Region, its crypt was consecrated by Urban II who, in the 1098, held a concile there in order to summon people to participate in the first crusade proclaimed by himself, and on the crypt itself rose the building, closed by a series of courtyards where markets took place, above all during the pilgrimages to the Holy Land, from which Bari got considerable wealths.

The simple front reveals a careful eye a series of precious mullioned windows with one and two lights, besides the portals with images of animals which, on the whole, produce lightness in the whole. Behind, the basilica with three aisles, being stately for the bareness of its parts and colonnades, reveals on the top a wooden ceiling in Seicento style with paintings by Carlo Rosa,which represent what only remains of the sumptuous Baroque decoration which in the past had covered the church, later destroyed by the restorations during the fifties and the sixties. Besides the iconostasis, which separates the nave from the transept, we can admire the series of Romanesque precious sculptures which make up Elia's pulpit (the first abbot and founder) and the ciborium which express the highest point of the art of that time through the preciousness of the capitals and figured animals as they were made by a goldsmith. In the basin of the apse there is the marble sarcophagus of Bona Sforza, Queen of Polony and Duchess of Bari who was a great benefactress of the Basilica (16th century) increasing its feudal powers. Below, the great crypt, extending under the transept, preserves the body of the Saint who has always been worshipped both in the West and in the East.

Outside, it is the whole building, not only its front which shows a rich and wonderful work of art, on the left side where mullioned windows with six lights with engraved capitals correspond, on the same level of women's gallery to a series of deep arcades, while the side door c.d. of Lions is worth reading in its sculptures by Basilio. Of four original bell towers only the two fore ones remain with a series of windows which make the building seem lighter up.

As this building is very famous, many people by mistake think this is the Cathedral of Bari, while the latter, devoted to St. Sabino is not very far from the former, in Odegitria square. Built about 1170, it rises on the place of the ancient Cathedral which was demolished in 1165 during the destruction of Bari, but more ancient traces have been brought to light from a wide mosaic floor (8th-9th centuries) discovered under the trampling level and probably referring back to a Palaeochristian basilica. The three-aisle inside was also object of restoration in the sixties, and it is divided by a double row of eight very thin columns which make it again a building with only a room. On the left side there are either the bell tower, in the hinder corner, or the "Trulla" ritual remains of a Byzantine tradition originally used as a baptistery for immersion and later as a vestry.

Of a particular sculptural value is the big window of the apse (12th century) placed on a flat wall which hides the three apses on the top of the ciborium, the latter reconstructed through the pieces of the original one.

From the square before the Cathedral we can see the foreshortening of the Swabian Castle, built in its original plan, by Frederick II, with a side on the sea which went on staying there even in the 16th century when Bona Sforza, making it her own sumptuous house, decided to fortify it with buttresses in the two corners leading to the land. The mighty castle, now seat of Superintendence of Cultural Good, was fortified with four square towers covered with dark "carparo" (a typical building material) later used as Borboun prison and barracks.

But Bari is not only represented by these three famous monuments or by the labyrinth of the streets of its old part,it is also rich in more modern buildings. Its very active centre is the place of trade like in the past and it is in the area of the suburb where stands out a series of buildings including Neoclassical and modern styles, being often seats of cultural institutions: from theatres (N. Piccini, Margherita, Petruzzelli) to University Palace (Archaeological Museum), etc...

The administrative functions, on the contrary, are

Bari, the front of the Basilica
of St. Nicola

Bari, the crypt of St. Nicola

on the way of the Promenade, one of the longest and most beautiful in Italy, result of an intense building period between the two wars when Araldo of Crollalanza from Bari became Minister of Public Works; one of the most accomplished achievements of the Fascist architecture applied to the town on a vast scale.

Here we can see the main buildings for entertaiment built in the twenties and thirties of this century which are the expression of the transformations of the aspect of Bari during this period of twenty years.

On the promenade of Levante we find Nations Hotel (1932-1935), planned by the Roman architect Alberto Calza Bini, the palace of Province designed by the engineer Luigi Baffa, the palace of Ministry of Public Works achieved by the Roman architect Carlo Vannoni between 1932 and '34, the barracks of the headquarters of the Third Air Region planned and completed in 1935 by the architects Aldo Forcignanò and Saverio Dioguardi and "Bergia" the barracks of carabineers in '36 thanks to the architect Cesare Bazzani. In the area of Levante, just in the inside, we find the Neo-Romanesque palace of Apulian Aqueduct planned and completed in 1932 by the architect C.Brunetti from Ravenna.

On Vittorio Veneto Promenade we find the Palace of Ministry of Finance (1934), the house of cripple

Bari, the Castle

achieved in 1935–40 according to the plan of the architect Pietro Favia, the two schools planned by the architect Concezio Petrucci, (Orazio Flacco Liceo and Institute of Commercial Sciences), as well as the barracks of the "voluntary troops for national security" by the architect Saverio Dioguardi.

Taking the way again towards Taranto, after a typical area of awning vineyards, we find Rutigliano, a medieval village in whose area various towns flourished in the past such as Azetium, Apulian and later Roman centre mentioned in Tabula Peuntigeriana and in Ravenna's itinerary which has brought to light many tombs with archaeological material dating back from 6th to 3rd centuries BC.

Equally important is the area of Bigetti where the small church of St. Apollinare (11th –12th centuries) rises and has revealed a series of necropolises with tombs rich in furnishings dating back from the 6th century BC. to the Longobard Middle Age.

On the ancient circle-shaped town, a mighty square tower in ashlar-work, thirty-four metres high (one of the most preserved towers in the area of Bari) completed on the top by a cornice jutting out with small arches with corbels. We can enter it from Cesare Battisti square which shows, on the opposite side, De Franceschis Palace, which includes the base of a circu-

Bari, detail of Palazzo Fizzarotti

lar tower crowned with an exedra.

If we keep going towards the right side, we will find the wonderful Renaissance portico of Antonelli palace and in the street which turns right, following the development of the first inside part of the town-walls, we will find Gonnella palace (1957) with a various ashlar-works (rough-hewn, cushioned, diamond-shaped) according to building levels and crowned with small arcades with a flower in the middle. Walking around the great palace placed on the other side, we will reach Roma street where the 18th century widening well harmonizes with De Laurentiis palace whose portal has a balcony in Andalusian style

on its top.

The cathedral of St. Mary of Column appears in the square at the end of the way. Already existing in 1059 and built in honour of Nullius Dioecesis by the Norman count Ugo in 1108, it was later widened and renewed more times. The porch keeps the sculptured architrave (Christ and the Apostles, and above, the Annunciation) of the first construction and the ogival archivolt on small columns resting on lions, dating back to 13th century. On the right side of the front, the high bell tower with mullioned windows with three lights has a Baroque clock on its top. The inside with three aisles keeps some pillars with very near half-columns; the church has got a poliptych by Antonio Vivarini, a 13th century Madonna of Byzantine influence, a whole collection of paintings by Carella set in the Baroque stuccoes, as well as many wooden sculptures in Cinquecento style. In addition to some fragments of Renaissance frescoes, the part of the apse in a valuable Neoclassical style achieved by the architect A. Pesce in 1832 is very interesting.

Passing the cathedral, we will reach a large square with Porta Nuova in the background inserted in Pappalepore palace with an arched entry in Settecento style with twin columns which opened in a beautiful inside entrance-hall.

Outside the town, taking the road to Turi, we can see at first the mighty convent of Madonna of Palace already belonging to the Observant Minorites, which is now under repair and then, before following the direction for Conversano (towards Casamassima), we can admire the fortified farmhouse of Panicelli (at the end of 16th century), a particular example of the interpretation of the theme in the shape of a fortified castle in miniature and with a draw bridge on the first floor.

Conversano, placed on a height which can be seen even from afar, overlooks a large part of the Adriatic coast. The Norman Conquest represents, after the Longobard and Byzantine short period, a turning point for the town with the reinforcement of the wide and jointed castle, the result of additions and changes between the 15th and 17th centuries. It has been the place of life of the powerful family of the counts Acquaviva d'Aragona (1456-1806), a period of remarkable splendour of the whole town as we can notice in many noble residences of that time spread throughout the old part of the town. The Castle's inside, partly belonging to private people, is enriched with Baroque frescoes by Finoglio.

In the same "largo di corte" (open space in the courtyard) from which we can enter the castle and the town-park, the bishop's palace and the area of the apse of the late Romanesque Cathedral appear, the latter already founded between the 11th and 12th centuries, it has suffered great restoration works, after the fire of 1911, thanks to Sante Simone who reconstructed the whole northern side.

The structure of St. Benedetto, in the homonymous street, is worth pointing out, seat of an ancient Benedictine monastery where the Cistercian nuns, taking the place of the friars in 1266, have governed for ages with feudal and episcopal privileges; inside there is the seat of Civic Museum. And we can't forget the church of Ss. Cosma and Damiano, a real jewel, a rare exmple of holy building which preserves an original Baroque image according to Acquaviva family's will as their own emblem; Cesare Fracanzano and Paolo Finoglia worked here.

In the country there is the interesting and very small church of St. Caterina (12th century) whose rich plan, taking inspiration from Syria, would bear witness to the relations of these quarters with the East during the crusades' time.

Even the great monastery of St. Mary dell'Isola (of the Isle) must be visited, with one of the two inside cloisters enriched with frescoes and with the church which hosts the sumptuous funeral monument of Acquaviva family dating back to the Renaissance (1480 cc.).

Coming back to the coast towards Polignano we are attracted by a suggestive rocky spur where an ancient village is riflected in the crystal-clear waters, where the white houses standing out against a continuously blue sky create a fabulous atmosphere, where the water decomposes light in a thousand colours which are reflected in the inside of so many natural caves being dug out in the rock. The most famous is surely the Palazzase one which can be visited as it has been transformed into a restaurant.

But the compactness of the place is covered in the inside, among the houses, with tortuous lanes which pierce arches, where people climb up steps or doze on beautiful porticoes on the sea.

We must visit the cathedral (at the end of the 13th century), seat of an ancient diocese, which keeps a precious polyptych by Bartolomeo Vivarini, sign of the relations with Venice, a stone crib in Cinquecento style sculptured by Stefano from Putignano, as well as a beautiful inlaid wooden pulpit belonging to the 16th century.

If we keep going southwards, we will find the small town of Monopoli with a very important strategic port and an age-long commercial activity, above all for the oils, which made it a feud of Venice, and, anyhow, its reference point between the 15th and 16th centuries. According to tradition, it is probably heir to the nearby Egnazia, placed on the coast further south

Polignano

and destroyed during the early Middle Ages, but more recent archaeological finds confirm the pre-existence, in the same place, of more ancient traces of an Apulian settlement.

Leaving from the 19th-century great square dedicated to Vittorio Emanuele we reach the old town; passing Plebiscito square with the town-hall and the Baroque church of St. Francesco, we can visit the church of St. Domenico, in the homonymous street, with a beautiful Renaissance tripartite front and enriched with statues attributed to Stefano from Putignano, in the inside a painting by Palma the Younger, another painting by the same painter is in the Cathedral, situated in an almost hidden position at the end of the street beyond XX September square, whose Baroque front (18th century) has got a very small square opposite to it which emphasises the imposing size of the church.

The inside with the plan of a basilica with three aisles is magnificently decorated with polychrome marbles, being more often valuable stuccoes which imitate it, with various works of art of famous artists such as: C. Rosa, De Mura, Marco from Siena, Bardellino, Lama, etc.; we must also visit the rooms of treasure and a series of remains of tombstones probably dating back to the original construction of 1107.

We must shortly visit the church of St. Mary from Amalfi, a small but precious Norman building, built on one of so many existing caves used by friars worshipping St. Basilio in the old part of the town. The latter was founded by a colony of people from Amalfi who inhabited here for commercial purposes. Of the three apses, above all the central one shows a beautiful window enriched with 13th-century sculptural ornaments.

The Caves of Castellana are surely worth visiting, they are an unusual and unexpected sight, placed outside the homonymous village; even if they have been known and used since ancient times, though they haven't been explored, they were better known and studied at the end of the 18th century. In modern age they became important after the rediscovery, resulting from an investigation on this spot by prof. Anelli, in 1938, of the Caves themselves which have nothing to envy of similar and more famous caves in other places of Italy.

Then we reach Alberobello, after taking the coastal road which winds along the fields of Valley of Itria, rich not only in olive- and almond-trees, but also typical stone buildings, the so-called "Trulli" for which the town is very famous in the world. Here we can't come only to visit a monument, be it a church, be it a castle, but all the area is a monument dedicated to the unceasing activity of man who has changed the territory cleverly using the same natural elements the land offered to him. A landscape where the remains of woods are well integrated with the traditional cultivations, where the "trulli" and the small houses emphasise with their whiteness the widespread red colour of land, also used itself in construction works as a linking element.

The origins are mysterious for a territory at the centre of conflicts between feudatories (Acquaviva family from Conversano) and the nearby towns such as: Martina Franca and Monopoli. Besides, we must remember the cathedral devoted to Ss. Cosma and

Damiano and the neoclassical monumental Cemetery achieved through the plan of the architect Curri.

On the other side of the valley rises Locorotondo whose place-name points out a feature which is obvious for those who reach here: the plan with the shape of a circle we still see along Nardelli street, a wide part of street where the close sequence of white houses, with their two-pitch roofs, follows the points of an ideal circle creating a suggestive scenographical effect.

After visiting quietly the streets of the ancient

Alberobello, the Siamese trullo

part, we must go to the neoclassical cathedral of St. Giorgio, built like many others, on previous buildings to one of which a group of stony sculptures, set in pillars and of evident Gothic influences would probably belong. Even the church of Madonna della Greca (of Greek) can date back to the same period (15th century), with three-aisle plan, closed by a front which, originally austere, then it has been, in an irremediable way, compromised by a copy of a Romanesque rose window put on the top of the front itself.

On the other side of the valley stands out Martina Franca, one of the most beautiful towns of art, not only in the Province of Taranto but in the whole Apulia.

Coming back towards Alberobello and Noci, we will reach Gioia Del Colle, the ancient Joha, already existing in Byzantine Age and overlooked, since the Middle Ages, by the dark bulk of its very beautiful Frederick's Castle. As a matter of fact, the austere quadrangular building, realized in ashlar of red "carparo" and well framed in the most important architectural elements, was founded by Riccardo Siniscalco at the end of 11th century and widened by King Roger; the intervention of the Swabian emperor in 1230 surely gave the final aspect to the building, object of a stylistic restoration of 1909 thanks to the architect Angelo

Trulli, decorations on the pinnacles

Pantaleo. The latter not only has invented the main mullioned window with three lights but he has also reconstructed a Hall of the Throne with pieces of stone coming from different rescues. Today, the castle with mighty square towers is the seat of Library and National Museum where there are the archaeological finds of the area of Gioia Del Colle.

On the outskirts, in Putignano street, there are the excavations of Mount Sannace which, opened at the end of the fifties, have revealed a great Apulian settlement protected by five circuits of town walls. It is one of the most important active centres in Peucezia, whose name is unknown, certainly existed in prehistorical age, but which reveals its highest splendour between the 6th and the 4th centuries b. C.

We reach Altamura after passing the high and stony Murgia; here we are not so far from the ancient route of the Appian Way. The wide ancient built-up area, which is influenced by the altimetrical location in its own circular formation, is still so much populated that it gives the clear impression of a break between the new and the old part of the town.

If the town of Peucezia was the first real built-up area of Altamura, it is due to the Emperor Frederick II the revival of the town through the building of a castle, the respective circuit of walls and the cathedral (1232). This is the magnificent and complex building, devoted to Our lady of Assumption in which more styles blend harmoniously and they represent a whole thanks to the 19th century building works of the

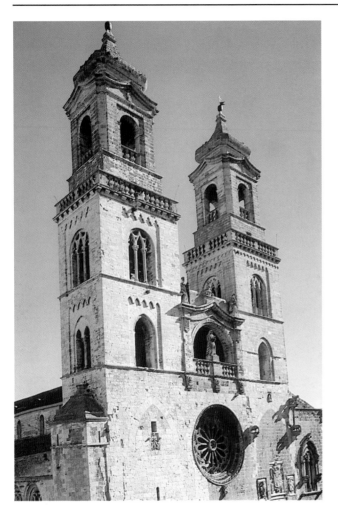

Neapolitan architect Travaglini. On the contrary, the exterior keeps a medieval trace where a 14th century rose window stands out in the austere front overlooked by two imposing bell towers, while the portal is richly decorated and it still keeps the representation of the Last Supper.

The original width of the space within the Swabian walls, has allowed the town, till the end of the 18th century, to develop buildings traditionally organized in "claustri", a urban typology with a close court, singular and typical of the town, probably linked to the presence of many people of different origins since the birth of the town itself. It is also witnessed by the ancient church of St. Nicolò of the Greeks, already built at the end of the 13th century in the place of a great Latin cathedral, for the population of Greek religion (being active till the 17th century).

Entering Bari Gate, a unique construction together with the palace of Del Balzo family and running straight into Corso Frederick II, we can see, besides Republic Square, the 19th century Town Hall, built after the Unity of Italy, in the area of the convent of St. Francesco, while if we go on, we will find, on left, the church of St. Nicolò and that of St. Biagio which shows the great ferryman of souls, St. Cristoforo on the front. In the middle of the town, Cathedral Square comprehends a series of palaces with rich and different open galleries which are opposite to the Tower of clock achieved through the plan of the architect De Judicibus in 1858.

Going on towards the main street beyond Matera Gate, we will reach the Civic Museum and the Library which preserves a collection of more than sixty thousand publications besides a collection of various archaeological pieces; not far from it, Mercadante theatre, devoted to the famous musician who was born here.

After Altamura we wouldn't expect, but for the premonitory name, to find a town on the brink of a ravine whose aspect is very similar to the nearby and more famous Matera. Today Gravina (Ravine) of Apulia is heir to a rocky civilization which, beyond the Roman Silvium marked in the Tabula Peutingeriana, is confined to so many caves and to the suggestive scenes of the ravine. With regard to it, it is advisable to visit the church of St. Michele, the ancient cathedral of the hypogeal (underground) town completely dug out in the rock, where we can arrive here from St. John wharf, with remains of frescoes on the walls, above we find the superior church devoted to St. Marco.

Gravina, the front of the church of Madonna delle Grazie

The conquest of the first Normans, the passage from Greek rite to Latin one, and the construction of the cathedral mark further development of the town followed by the establishment of a great hunting castle for Frederick II's will, as well as the very ancient fair (1313) organized by Roberto d'Angiò.

Reaching notar Domenico square we can see the Church of Purgatory ordered to be built by Orsini family (feudatories from 1420 to 1807) as family's chapel (we must notice the bears on the portal's columns) which keeps pictorial decorations by Francesco Guarino, completed, after his death, by Angelo Solimena in the second half of the 17th century. In the same square devoted to Benedetto XIII (who became Pope from 1724) the side front of the Cathedral appears; it was reconstructed, after the fire, in the second half of the 15th century with the help of Dalmatian masters probably commissioned by the duchess Angela Castriota Scandemberg, whose beautiful sepulchre is kept in the church of St. Sofia. While the exterior keeps an elegant simpleness, typical of Renaissance, the inside is enriched with a series of works of art among which stands out the golden and gilt wooden ceiling.

If we come back to the first small square and we go around the corner of the small church of Purgatory, after two light diversions we will reach Pomarici-Santomasi palace (17th century) where, besides the rich archaeological collection and the museum, we can see the reconstruction of the rocky church of St. Vito the old, rich in frescoes of Byzantine influence accomplished by local painters.

Very particular is the church of Madonna delle Grazie (of Graces) placed, beyond the railway station, at the end of Lettieri street where the front appears imposing and representing an eagle with three towers which is the heraldic emblem of monsignor Giustiniani, the commissioner of itself. Coming back to the old part of the town, we will find, on left half-way, the magnificent neoclassical palace of Gramegna brothers with a wide colonnade and in the inside a well-shaped staircase at the end of the main courtyard.

In order to finish the visit, it is advisable to come back to the beginning of the street and visit the suggestive ravine going down the Star Fountain street and see the rocky churches of St. Mary of Angels and Madonna of the Star.

Alberobello

The province of Brindisi

The province of Brindisi was created, as Benito Mussolini himself said, to suit this land to the yearning for expansion towards the Balkans on the part of the regime. The policy, which we also find in the books by Pasquale Camassa (1858-1941) represented almost as a spiritual motto, was that Brindisi, a strategic base of military operations in the East during the Roman Empire's time, had to play again this similar role with similar aims for expansion. However, Brindisi's port, at least sixty years before, was already included in the great international routes; the opening of the Suez Canal had made Brindisi's port even more important including it in the routes linking the United Kingdom with its colonies in Asia, Africa and Australia. During the First World War it had been a naval base of primary importance; here, besides, the Austro-Hungarians succeeded in exploding and sinking "Benedetto Brin" ironclad. In that situation the population had increased very quickly: in 1861 Brindisi had just 9.137 inhabitants; in 1901 it had more than doubled the number reaching 23.106 people and in 1931 it already almost reached 40.000 inhabitants. The new province, when the constitution was issued with Royal decree, law n. 1 of 2nd January1927, had 229.348 inhabitants altogether and it was extended for 179.432 hectares; therefore it was the smallest province in Apulia. The last one, nevertheless, but it was not the minor one: its territory was unanimously considered the most productive one in the Region. Brindisi has performed the functions of a leading town as it was at the head of the area, the so-called "circondario" (district) according to Bourbon denomination, comprehending the communes of Brindisi, Carovigno, Ceglie Messapica, Erchie, Francavilla Fontana, Guagnano, Latiano, Mesagne, Oria Ostuni, Salice Salentino, Sandonaci, San Pancrazio Salentino, San Vito dei Normanni, Torre Santa Susanna, Veglie and the villages of Villa Castelli and San Michele Salentino, being now communes. On the whole, they are sixteen communes and four hamlets extending in the area of Lecce and following in the south, except for Leverano, the borders of the archdiocese of Brindisi and in the north, except for Locorotondo, the borders of the archdiocese of Ostuni directed by the metropolitan bishops of Brindisi.

In 1927 this composition was changed as Guagnano, Salice and Veglie were excluded and assigned to Lecce and San Pietro Vernotico, Torchiarolo and Cellino San Marco, on the contrary, were separated from their old "circondario".

In the north, the new province recovered Cisternino and Fasano, already belonging to the territory of Bari and it presented itself as an ideal meeting point between the two areas, that of the Salento and that of the centre of Apulia which had particular features and they often had different cultural references. The clear intention about the plan which had been pursued in the previous decades, was to create a mighty central area with the functions of leader in regional field, referring to the triangle made up of Bari-Brindisi-Taranto, a middle-point in comparison with the extreme points of the areas of Foggia and Lecce.

This situation should have given unity to the region; besides, soon after the unity of Italy, the union of important resources in three sea towns aimed at this policy. The sea towns are: Taranto, an important base of Navy, Brindisi, the final destination for trade beyond Suez and Bari, a centre of exchanges. It must be said that the plan has always been pursued, though in alternate phases (between the fifties and the sixties much money was invested in this area: it is enough to remember Montecatini oil-chemical industry in Brindisi and Italsider steel-plants in Taranto). It was proposed as an industrial triangle in the south in order to be competitive against the north which had its main points in Milan, Turin and Genoa.

The province of Brindisi, apparently heterogeneous when it rose, seems to have developed the sense of its own deep unity: the administrative borders follow the natural ones following the ridge of Premurge and, in the south, the marshes, now drained, which separated the Messapian plain of Lecce's Salento. About cultural level it is necessary to notice that the present territorial order seems to imitate, for the most part, the Messapian one; the fact that, in spite of the forced superimposition of populations and cultures, this basic situation has remained unchanged, justifies completely the return to the Messapian area, featured by Oria-Brindisi line, in the dimension of the province.

Brindisi. Leaving other possible references out of consideration, the settlement of Punta Le Terrare, on the east-side of the middle port, was thought to be linked to the protohistorical itineraries of amber and obsidian and considered one of the places attended by

A view from the sky of the port of Brindisi

Mycenaean people. The presence of a Corinthian column, whose clear traces were discovered in the last year in the area where a railway station was being constructed, bears witness to a phase in the relation between the two shores of the Adriatic which the arrival of Messapian people would get over. As a matter of fact, it is the military alliance with Athens which allows Brindisi to find a deterrent to the expansionism of Taranto towards the Adriatic. If we take again the small street of the plateau which looks out on the western bay, we will be able to recognize the Messapian urban plan which is evident from the rests on which stands out the town theatre and which show the use the Romans made for the second time. It is the inclusion itself of Brindisi in the Roman imperial structure which confers a new role on the port which, call of regional importance, becomes one of the main jointing points in international relations. Connected with Rome through the Appian Way, to which then the Traiana Way will be added, it will become the Adriatic call of more vital importance in the plan of the expansionism towards the east. The conversion to Christianity of these quarters which was complete only in the 5th century, included new reference points in the built-up area of Brindisi; in the necropolis of Cappuccini quarter there is the martyrium of St.

Brindisi, the Cathedral

Leucio, the great bishop who promoted the evangelization of Salento between the 4th and the 5th centuries, in the middle of the town the ecclesia mater, perhaps on the site of St. John al Sepolcro (to the Sepulchre), and the churches of St. Pelino and St. Mary, now only historical reminiscences. The destruction of the town by the Longobards coming from Benevento around 670, causes the transfer of the episcopal cathedral to Oria. The first attempt to rebuild the town happened in the 9th century thanks to Byzantium; the only result is perhaps the unfinished saying engraved on the base of the surviving column of the port. Only during the 11th century other supporters, the Normans will try the enterprise; acting according to fiscal pressure they will encourage the re-population in vetera civitate, on the western hill, where the new cathedral will rise after its consecration in 1089 by the Pope Urban II. Between the 11th and 12th centuries the structures of St. Maria Veterana or St. Benedetto and St. John to the Sepulchre are built or are planned again; in the countryside, under the jurisdiction of the monastery of St. Andrea in Insula there are the monastic settlements of St. Biagio a Jannuzzo and St. John a Cafaro. During Frederick's time the town, seat of one of the most important mints of the Reign, is defended by a new fortress, the castle of land, pivot of a new defensive perimeter of which only Mesagne Gate remains, through which the expansion of the built-up area was

Brindisi, the Alfonsine Castle

allowed on the plateau of east. In this sense, the ecclesiastical buildings of St. Lucia and Christ of Dominicans must be considered as reference point in the urban development. During the Angevin period, the town is greatly supported by the kings: St. Paul the Hermit of the Conventuals bears witness to it as it is in the sphere of interest of the princes of Taranto who pretend to be extremely generous towards the church of St. Mary of Casale, summer residence of the archbishops of Brindisi. In the 15th century the Aragonese kings encourage, still acting on fiscal pressure, the re-population of the town, devastated by civil conflicts. So the modernization of the defensive system begins to be carried out above all because of the growing threat: Turkish at the entrance of the port the Alfonsine castle is built, the castle of land is widened, new town-walls are planned reviving the layout of the town during Frederick's time. The Aragonese plan will be completely defined during the vice-regal period with additions to the castle of land, the reconstruction of the fortress on the isle of St. Andrea, the plan or the remaking of the following towers: Guaceto, teste of Gallico, Punta Penne, Capo Cavallo and Mattarelle on the coastline. The new great line of the roads which joins Mesagne Gate to Royal Gate, in the port, crossing the other one which goes from Lecce Gate towards St. Paolo the Hermit, determines a new arrangement of urban space; the centre of the town,

Brindisi, the isle of St. Andrea, entrance to the Fortress

for ages lying on the line which had the Cathedral and St. Benedetto as the two opposite sides, moves southwards. At the meeting point of the new ways leading to the gates of the town, the church of St. Mary of Angels will rise at the beginning of the 17th century.

There were new possibilities for Brindisi during the 18th century in the different situation caused by the crisis of the Ottoman Empire; it will be necessary to wait about a century, through alternate events determined by clear wrongs in the plans and construction works, to see the development of commercial activities of the port which finally will become a call for trade beyond Suez with the arrival of the" Valigie delle Indie" in Brindisi. In this period, in the second half of the 19th century, a new line of roads substitutes the Spanish one and it is made up of the road which joins the railway station to the port. During the First World War there is the emphasis on the military potentialities of the roadstead; from Brindisi, Paolo Thaon of Revel, commander-in-chief of the mobilized naval strength, directed the military operations of Navy throughout the war period. This role is emphasized by the decision to build here the Monument to the Mariner of Italy, unveild on 4th November, in 1933 by King Vittorio Emanuele II. Ten years later, on

other circumstances, the King would come back, making the town, capital of the Reign, from the September of 1943 to the February of 1944.

From Brindisi, through the Salentine coastline, passing along the area of salt-pans.

From Brindisi we can reach Torchiarolo; the front of the Cathedral devoted to Our Lady, the Virgin Mary received into Heaven belongs to the 18th century. The baronial palace, like many others in the province, was originally only a tower which we can still identify in the right side of the building. The transformation from a military structure to a civil residence was here slower than elsewhere as the town was very exposed to sea attacks and its evolution was achieved only at the end of the 17th century. In Torchiarolo the houses seemed fortresses; the still existing one in Prince Amedeo street has got an entry being defended by an embrasure. In the countryside there is the sanctuary of Santa Maria di Galeano in which there is Her miraculously saved image.

Between Torchiarolo and San Pietro Vernotico there are the ruins of Valesio of which wide parts of the Messapian town-walls can still be seen. Besides, there was a spa whose first exploration was achieved in 1960 by Gabriele Marzano.

San Pietro Vernotico has in the towers the most evident signs of the long feudal domination on the part of the bishops from Lecce. Around it, developed both residential and administrative buildings, warehouses and baronial mills on whose site the Town Hall of People square will be built, or ecclesiastical buildings including the church of Our Lady, the Virgin Mary received into Heaven. The tower is probably similar to those of hamlets, it will be enough to mention the towers of the nearby Torchiarolo and Tuturano and the ones of the rural settlements. It has a square base with crenellations and embrasures and on the whole it dates back to the 16th century considering its present aspect; in that period there were constructions based on a late 14th century plan, probably in the project of reviewing the defensive system of the

reign on the Adriatic, which so concretely defeated the fears of the population who felt undefended before the attacks of the enemies.

At a short distance from San Pietro Vernotico there is Cellino San Marco; the small town had its first high medieval cultural reference in its sanctuary of St. Marco considered as a middle point of conflicts between Longobards and Byzantines in Salento and at the edges of Oria-Otranto route. The consequent success of the worship for St. Marco was due to the interests of people from Veneto in this area as we can notice from an altar devoted to St. Marco by themselves in the church; the final assertion of the worship for

The archaeological area of Valesio

St. Marco occurred at the beginning of the 18th century when the sanctuary of the Saint was rebuilt because of a renewed presence of man in this territory. Of the original structure of the count's palace only a stone balustrade with round pillars over the porch remains.

San Donaci has the important monument in the church of St. Miserino, in Monticello quarter, with a central plan with four small opposite apses and three flat-bottomed arches. The dome-shaped covering is in opus caementicium. We can enter the central room through a pronaos between two small rooms where there are traces of stucco works. Its exterior has a quadrangular shape. It dates back from the 6th to the 7th

centuries. The church has been thought to have been used in the past as a "ninfeo" (a small temple devoted to nymphs) and during the Byzantine time transformed into a building for Christian worship, probably a baptistery.

San Pancrazio Salentino keeps in the church of St. Anthony the memorial iconographical image of the Turkish assault in 1547: according to Girolamo Marciano's tale, five Ottoman galleons, on 1st January night, landed at Columena Tower where a group of plunderers led by a renegade from Avetrana, a certain Chria got ashore. The latter led them as far as San Pancrazio which was caught as completely undefen-

Mesagne, Archaeological Museum. Bell and volute crater, found out in the Prince's Tomb

ded: almost all the inhabitants were captured, carried to Turkey and sold as slaves. The town owes its reconstruction and re-population to the small feudataries of Brindisi who, in the 16th centuries considered it as their summer residence that is why they took care of the castle, now being in very low conditions. In the countryside there is the sanctuary of St. Anthony from Padua, already St. Anthony the Abbot, developed on previous Medieval buildings: as a matter of fact it comprehends a cave with wall pictures and an adjoining anchoretic centre.

From San Pancrazio we can reach Mesagne; along the road, in Malvindi quarter, we can visit a Roman spa. Going on we will find the remains of the Messapian centre of Muro Maurizio where we can still see part of the town walls. In Mesagne the Civic Museum bears witness to classical and pre-classical events of the town. The latter has been supported by Madonna del Carmine whose worship was forstered by Her believers who settled in Mesagne in 1521 taking possession of the royal abbey of St. Michele Arcangelo. In the church, now devoted to the Virgin, a great devotion was bestowed on the image painted by Francesco Palvisino from Putignano after the arrival of the friars into the town. The cathedral, devoted to All Saints, was built between 1650 and 1660, when

St. Eleuterio, whose statue dominates the entry, was still the main patron of the town. The church of St. Mary of Bethlehem, belonging to Celestines till 1807, whose convent is today the municipal seat, was rebuilt in 1738 using, as Rosario Jurlaro says "askew the area of a more ancient church of 1528". Of early Middle Ages is the church of St. Lorenzo outside the walls, having three aisles whose apse has a mullioned window with three lights, built in opus quadratum, with multiple measures of the Roman foot, between the 6th and 7th centuries. The castle probably created thanks to the Normans, was finally redefined by Giovanni Antonio del Balzo-Orsini, prince of Taranto,

about 1430. Between the 17th and 18th centuries, thanks to the changes and additions wished at first by Giovanni Antonio Albricci and then by Ignazio Barretta, lords of Mesagne, it took more a residential aspect than military one.

From Mesagne we can go towards Torre (Tower) Santa Susanna ; along the way there is the church of St. Peter of Crepacore, at the edges of the very ancient road which from Taranto, passing through Oria, led to Valesio. In early Middle Ages, this road was perhaps included in the artery which went down towards Otranto as the Traiana Way of the Romans also did. The church of St. Peter was built before the 9th century and it showed the quadrilateral space with an eighteen foot side, that is equivalent to the initials Jn of the Holy Name. Before this space there was a hall which was covered in Norman age; on the sides there are two small aisles, that of more ancient part is divided by two square pillars, the others are divided by the drums of a Roman fluted marble column. For its position near to the early Middle Ages border between Byzantines and Longobards the church has been thought to be built as a castrensian church. Torre (Tower) Santa Susanna has a very important castle for the feudatory Tiberio Dormio's wish in 1588 and it was much changed in the following century emphasizing more the military function than the residential one. The Sanctuary of St. Mary of Galaso preserves the image of Mary which is supposed to be miraculously found in 1481 in the well we can still see behind the high altar. In the last altar of the right side there is the Nativity, relief sculptured and wash painted by Gabriele Riccardi from Lecce in 1588. The cathedral, devoted to the Virgin, St. Nicola and St. Susanna was built in 1581 "over a more ancient architectural scheme, already tried in the cathedral of Ostuni" and in the cathedral of Latiano.

In Erchie, Laviano family, dukes of Satriano and marquises of Tito, inhabited the 18th century palace to whose plan, at least regarding the North wing, the great architect Francesco Milizia should have contributed. A national monument is the hypogeal (underground) church of the Virgin Mary, of high importance, as Jurlaro said, for the structure of its entry "hollowed out like the dromos of prehistorical tombs, in the rock and limited above with megalithic walls inclined towards the inside and covered with hewn stones placed horizontally". The sanctuary of St. Lucia was built over a water-spring which was considered to be effective in the cure for many diseases of eyes.

From Erchie, stopping at the sanctuary of St. Cosimo alla Macchia where pilgrims arrive here from the nearby villages on Wednesdays and Thursdays in the fifth week after Easter, we can reach Oria. Its castle is one of the best preserved in the region. Frederick II is supposed to have encouraged the construction or the reconstruction; the square tower, in the south-western corner seems to have been built before the others of the "sperone", in the North, of "Cavaliere", in the South, and of the "Salto", in the South-Eastern top which can be supposed to be of Angevin origins. The church of Ss. Crisanto and Dauria is under the hall of the castle and its planimetrical system reproduces in very reduced sizes, that of the basilica of St. Marco in Venice. It was built by the bishop Teodosio, to place the corps of Saints Martyrs Crisanto and Daria, at the end of the 9th century, when they were discovered in Rome. We must point out that the squares' covering is the first pattern of tholos building in Apulia, later widely used for "trulli". The church of the Palestinian hermit St. Barsanofrio, Oria's patron since the end of the 9th century, the age during which His relics were transformed, is hollowed out in the rock outside the walls, from the side of Judea and in front of Iris hill. Before receiving the relics, it was devoted to St. Anthony the Abbot. On the left side of the superior church, built between 1579 and 1580 and since the 18th century devoted to St. Francesco of Paola, there is a piece of sarcophagus which, drawn out of the ruins of the mortuary chapel ordered to be built by the bishop Teodosio to place there the relics of the Saint, was used again in the 16th century as architrave for a portal which was later closed. The hermitical church of Santa Maria della Scala, in the area of Salinelle, in the middle of a destroyed anchoretic settlement, has been thought to date back to the 14th century.

The diocese of Oria comprehending Oria, Avetrana, Ceglie Messapica, Erchie, Francavilla Fontana, Latiano, Manduria, Maruggio, Sava, Torre Santa Susanna, Uggiano Montefusco, Villa Castelli, was established on the 10th of May, 1591 separating the diocese itself from that of Brindisi and making it suffragan to Taranto. It has its reference point in the Cathedral basilica, rebuilt in the place of the previous one of Romanesque age, between 1750 and 1756. In the episcopal palace there are remarkable frescoes, attributed to the school of Pellegrino Tibaldi (1527-96) which are, according to Vincenzo Pugliese, "the most beautiful and, for some reasons, particular manneristical decoration achieved in Apulia".

From Oria, leaving the gate of the Hebrews or that of Manfred, both of them rebuilt in the 18th century, we can go towards Latiano; along the road we can stop at Santa Maria di Gallana, built in the 6th century in opus listatum with multiple sizes of Roman foot, being already a basilica with three aisles. The aisles' covering was barrel one, in opus caementicium as the right-side space transformed into warehouse shows clearly. The church, placed on the stretch between Oria and Scamnum of the ancient Appian Way shows square spaces with "trullo" covering and which can be attributed to a remaking of the 9th or 10th centuries.

In the neighbourhood of Latiano there is the sanctuary of St. Mary of Cotrino, already existing in 1565, widened in 1785, restored in the second half of the 19th century and since 20th August, 1922 place of life for the Cistercian monks. Symbol of civil power, now seat of the town hall, originally it must have been only a small fortress; the two towers which we can see in Spinelli street, probably contemporary to the other one of Solise in St. Margherita street seem to date back to the 16th century. At the end of the 17th century, the residence of feudatories develops around the two towers; like many other castles of the province, that of Latiano changes from a defensive building into a structure representing the power of Lords. The works which gave the structure an almost defined aspect happened in 1724 probably due to the architect Mauro Manieri. In Latiano there is the museum of Arts and Traditions, opened on the 13th December 1974 and later widened with some rooms dedicated to pottery in Apulia; there has also been the rebuilding of needlework and housework rooms.

The main building for worship is the cathedral which, rebuilt between the last years of the 15th century and the first ones of the following century, for the remake during this century, can be said to keep the light of the original rose window as the only primitive element. In the neighbourhood of Latiano, in the countryside of Mesagne, there are the remains of Scamnum, now called Muro Tenente. They belong to a Messapian built-up area of which we can see some parts of town-walls and of the necropolis. In the district of Grottole there is the cave church of St. John with traces of wall paintings of 13th and 14th centuries.

From Latiano we can easily reach Francavilla Fontana, whose foundations was probably due to Filippo, prince of Taranto, in 1310; the family who has left its own marks on the town more than others is that of Imperiali, lords of the town from 1572 to 1582. Their residence, now seat of the town hall, is one of the most important buildings in Salento; originally it was only a tower ordered to be built by the prince of Taranto, Giovanni Antonio Orsini del Balzo at the beginning of the 15th century; then the marquis Giovanni Bernardino Bonifacio added other two towers giving it the aspect of a fortress. The Imperiali themselves gave the present plan of the structure, with twenty wide windows and two large courtyards, from one of which the staircase leading to private rooms starts. The eastern gallery was sculptured by artists from Lecce in the half of the 17th century; the northern porch could be attributed to the architect Mauro Manieri who, in 1473, took part in the plan of the Cathedral. New works were achieved between 1701 and 1730 through the plans coming from Rome; very important is the picture-gallery of the family which has been still partly preserved. Now the collections also comprehend works of art coming from the abolished convents; the picture-gallery of Francavilla is the most important of the province till the diocesan museum of Brindisi develops definitely. The cathedral was built in the place where the miraculous image of Maria Santissima della Fontana is thought to have been discovered on the 14th September, 1310. Either the icon or the spring from which, the deer which had caused the discovery had watered, were in the crypt; nevertheless the fresco was detached to be placed in the superior church, in 1613. As the whole building was destroyed by the earthquake of 20th February 1743, it was rebuilt and completed in 1759. The churches of St. Mary of Cross, with a 13th century fresco representing Mary, of the Holy Spirit started to be built on the 19th March 1759, of the Immaculate, completed in 1867 and consecrated two years later, bear witness to the development of the local architecture from previous Medieval style to Neoclassic one.

About civil architecture it is necessary to mention at least Bianco palace, in Francesca Forleo Brajda street, Bottari, in Umberto I street, Pepe palace, in Regina Elena street and Barbaro Forleo villa, on the road for Manduria, built at the beginning of the last century. Of the gates of the town, that of Carmine was built in 1640, that of Capuchins in the 18th century, the other of Cross in 1714.

Villa Castelli was a hamlet of Francavilla Fontana till 1926, when it got the municipal freedom; the cathedral overlooks here, completed in 1742 according to traditional patterns with Romanesque, Gothic and Baroque references. In the small town there are very few testimonies to the houses of the first farmers, the so-called "trulli" of which few signs remain. The castle, now under repair, is seat of civic administration; it is a small fort which in the past was armed with two cannons, already belonging to Imperiali and then to Ungaro of Monteiasi family who summoned farmers from Ceglie Messapica and Grottaglie to turn the area into cultivation, still dominated by the maquis (bushes) during the last century.

In the countryside, along the road for Grottaglie, there is the settlement of Pezza Petrosa, with attendances witnessed from the end of the 5th century to the 3rd century BC., perhaps a Greek fortified outpost which is placed along the eastern boundaries of the "chora" of Taranto. Other ancient references are represented by the so-called "specchie" (mounds) for example that of Facciasquata which represent the most meaningful documents of the Messapian civilization, dating back to the period between the 6th and the 3rd centuries BC. The farmhouses such as: that of Mount Fellone, seem to be similar, for their whole architectural plan, to Northern-European patterns introduced here by the Irish monks who lived and practised their religion during the 7th century.

The nearby Ceglie Messapica is dominated by the imposing bulk of the fortress which was planned by Sanseverino family and built between the 15th and the 16th centuries on a previous building of Angevin age; in the walls planned in defence of the town there are the gate of Monterone, protected by a 15th century square tower and that of Giuso probably dating back

Cisternino

to the 13th century. The churches of St. Gioacchino and St. Rocco are of neoclassical style together with the unfinished town theatre; in the countryside, on the road for Francavilla, there are the "specchia" (mound) of Miano or Castelluzzo, perhaps the most archaic among the existing ones in the territory of Brindisi; the church of the Madonna of Cave, built in the 14th century and including a Karst cave with an image of Mary which is supposed to date back to the 13th century; the Karst cave of St. Michele where we find the most ancient image of Mary in the province as it has been attributed to the 8th century.

From Ceglie, through the valley of Itria, where "trulli" make the landscape very characteristic, we can reach Cisternino; in the cathedral, devoted to St. Nicola, the Madonna del Cardellino (of Goldfinch), by Stefano from Putignano, belonging to 1517 has been preserved. We can still see the Medieval defensive system; long parts of the town walls, the circular towers of Vento and of Amato and the square one of Bishop have been preserved. About civil buildings we point out the palace in Marconi square, of Baroque style.

Fasano was under the domination of the Knights of Malta; famous bailiffs were Alessandro Carafa,

Paola, ordered to be built by Leonardo Guerrieri.

Between Fasano and Monopoli there is the church of St. Peter lo Petraro (the Stone-worker), in the district of Seppannibale, the most interesting and perhaps the most ancient one among the churches of Apulia with lined domes.

In the sea there are the remains of Egnazia, episcopal seat, between the 5th and 6th centuries, built, as Horatio wrote "under the curse of aquatic nymphs" and where, according to Pliny, "there was a holy stone on which it was enough to put a wooden piece to cause a sudden rising of flame". The continuous excavations made in this area, have brought to light a paved road on the way of the Appian-Traiana which skirts the area of the forum; we can also see the foundations of some Christian basilicas with mosaic floors of the 5th and 6th centuries. In the countryside of Fasano we can notice the signs of the Medieval settlement around the monastic residences and cave churches all of them keeping frescoes, such as: Defence of Malta, Ottava, Pozzo (Well) Faceto, Sciurlicchio, Campranella, Lama Cupa, Laureto, St. Donato, St. Marco, St. Lorenzo, St. John, Lama d'Antico, St. Virgilia, Coccaro, St. Basilio St. Francesco, St. Nicola, Facianello, Seppannibale, Lamalunga, Saints Andrea and Procopio. In the hamlet of Pozzo Faceto there is the sanctuary of the Madonna del Pozzo (Well), already known in 1195. The territory, from the Wood to the resort of Torre Canne, a spa, also thanks to the presence of structures such as the zoo Safari, is very attended by tourist who stop here or only pass. The same situation happens in the resort of Ostuni with the settlements of Monticelli, Rosa Marina, Pilone, Villanova, Costa Merlata and Torre Pozzella.

Before reaching "the white queen of olive-trees", from Fasano, it is suitable to stop at Montalbano, where we find the dolmen, that is a tunnel tomb of the Bronze Age.

On the other hand, the territory of Ostuni, was

who in 1487 ordered the construction of the town-walls whose traces are in the cylindrical tower which still exists between St.Francesco and Dragone streets, and Fabrizio Francone, to whom incisive works on the Knights'palace in 1758 are attributed. Albano palace, in Corso Garibaldi, and the other ones, in Corso Vittorio Emanuele, corresponding to No. 77 and 81, bear witness to the development of the local Baroque architecture from imitative schemes to a language which "no longer conforms to grammatical and syntactical rules". The cathedral, with its Renaissance front, has completely reconstructed rooms dating back to the 18th century; church and convent of the Minims were built, in the first half of the 18th century, in the place of the 17th century church of San Francesco di

Ostuni

already attended by hunters of Neanderthal Age in the middle Paleolithic Age, about 50.000-40.000 years ago. As Donato Coppola has pointed out "in the higher Palaeolithic age there is a great deal of traces of human population; the burial, in the cave of St. Mary d'Agnano, of a twenty-year woman being on the point of bearing children dates back to 24.500 years ago. The corpse, pitifully placed in a big pit, was in a contracted position, with her hand under the head and the other, embellished with a shell bracelet, on her abdomen as she wanted to protect the baby; the head was covered with a red ochre and with a sort of bonnet with hundreds of small shells sewn on it. Her belonging to a group of hunters was proved by the remains of her outfit including flints and the teeth of horse and primitive ox. The foetus of the burial ground, called Ostuni 1° is unique throughout the world.

The museum of pre-classical civilizations of southern Murgia, in the ex convent of Monacelle, bears witness to these past ages because, also for its position in the middle of the ancient part of Ostuni, it lies in the place where a village of huts of Middle Bronze Age developed about the 16th-15th centuries BC. Near the museum there is the church of St. Vito, built in 1750-4, among the few Baroque patterns in Ostuni; in the neighbourhood we find the magnificent Cathedral. Ostuni was episcopal seat since the second half of the 11th century; in 1818 it was abolished and

the bishop Arpone kneeling at the foot of the Virgin on the Throne. Among many churches, we must mention at least that of the Virgin Mary; there are the remarkable panels of the 16th century choir and the frescoed vault of the chapel of the Crucified, with the images of the four Evangelists and of the Doctors of the Church and the church of the Holy Spirit, ordered to be built by the bishop Vincenzo Meligne in 1637, with a Renaissance porch and fan-light in relief of Dormitio Virginis belonging to the late 15th century.

About the civic building, we point out the neo-classical Jurleo palace, in the corner between Francesco Tanzarella-Vitale street and Corso Mazzini, planned by the architect Filippo Gaetano Jurleo (1860-1926). At the foot of Mount Morrone, along the "most beautiful hermitical path in Italy" there is the sanctuary of St. Oronzo, the patron of Ostuni; inside there is the cave where Oronzo is supposed to have stopped in order to escape the assassins hired by Nero. The rupestrian (rocky) settlement of St. Biagio in Ribaldo is not so far from here; on the 3rd February, for the celebration of the Saint, believers coming from all the villages of the area of Brindisi gather in the sanctuary. The settlements in the caves usually existed above all in the past, an example is that of St. Mary of Agnano; the caves with cultural functions have often changed their names, as in the example of Agnano where from the pagan sanctuary devoted to Great Mother there has been the change to that of God's Mother. The "masserie" (farmhouses) of the territory of Ostuni: Rialbo di Sopra, Carestia, Lo Spagnulo, Santa Caterina from the 16th to the 19th centuries, bear witness to the evolution of these factories which are essential for the dairy industry, for the supply of meats and the production of wool.

At a short distance from Ostuni, Carovigno lies "on the top of a delightful hill"; according to Salvatore Morelli "the ground, the climate, and the romantic sights differently fill the heart with a sublime pleasure". Of the pre-Roman town-walls, that we could still see in the last century, only the parts we can see

the territory was added to the archdiocese of Brindisi to which it was suffragan. It was re-established in 1821 and given to be administered to the archbishops of Brindisi. Through a present measure of abolition, it has been again united with Brindisi; its territory included Ostuni, Carovigno, Locorotondo, San Michele Salentino, San Vito dei Normanni.

The Cathedral began to be built during the episcopacy of Nicola Arpone (1437-70) and it was probably completed about 1520. The front is comparable with that of St. Mary Jemale in Milan; the inside, completely changed in the 17th century, has three aisles. In the fan-light of the major portal there is the image of

behind the new church remain. The Medieval defensive system, restored by Raimondo from Martina in 1527 has been better preserved. The castle, built at the end of the 15th century, is supposed to have been planned by Francesco di Giorgio Martini al least about what is concerned with the almond tower. The cathedral, completely restored in the last century, keeps on its front the rose window of the ancient one, built between the 15th and 16th centuries and, in the inside, the apse with ten niches arranged on two rows. On the road leading to the sea there is the sanctuary of St. Mary of Belvedere including a cave where we find the 14th century image of Mary and a Renaissance tabernacle by Giovanni Lombardo from Ostuni who was commissioned by Pirro de Loffreda to build it in 1501.

San Vito dei Normanni, already belonging to the Slavonians, or of Slavs, has its essential reference point in the castle. Originally it was only a tower which can be dated back to the Norman period and it was later completely transformed. It was particularly the baron Ottavio Serra, in the 17th century, who ordered to widen the castle so greatly that the fort took the aspect of a comfortable residence. In 1815 new, deep restoration works caused the change of the aspect of the structure: starting from the idea of the Middle Ages more than considering it in its real aspect, the structure was restored what was thought to be the original aspect of the castle. The cathedral began to be built in 1517, when people who had taken part in the battle of Lepanto, under the guide of Ruggero Danusci, came back to San Vito; a late 16th century painting, in the same church, bear witness to the announcement of victory of the Virgin over the Pope Pio V, next to which there is Ruggero Danusci. The Renaissance front, for the changes in 1773, is today the final part of the church. The old parish church, established in the 15th century, was widely renewed in 1763 when it was given its present aspect in its main features; the portal of the church of St. Teresa is of neoclassical style and ordered to be built by Salvatore Azzarito in 1827.

San Michele Salentino was the hamlet of San Vito till 1929, since then it has been an autonomous commune; the Cathedral can be considered sign of the identity of the town, built in the place of the one the prince Ernesto Dentice of Frasso had ordered to build in 1876 in Dante square; completed at the beginning of the forties, the new church expresses the wish to gather round symbols who didn't belong to the past. However, the territory doesn't seem to have been populated in recent age; in the countryside there are traces and sometimes many remains of Medieval settlements: this is the case of San Giacomo or, of more ancient ones probably pre-Roman settlements of Santa Maria della Selva.

On the straight road which from San Vito leads to Brindisi, a diversion is necessary to visit St. John a Cafaro and St. Biagio a Jannuzzo; the cave-church of St. John, hollowed out in the tufaceous rock, has a flat ceiling. There are votive frescoes and Latin inscriptions on the walls. It is included in a structure made up of four other semicircular caves which are connected with couches and niches hollowed out in the rock. The frescoes, except for two 15th century votive images, can probably date back to the 13th century.

The settlement of Jannuzzo develops around a height which, on the northern and eastern sides, is surrounded by the bends of a stream of water. Caves of different width are all around the cave-church. In these caves there are couches hollowed out in the rock, small niches and lamp-holders. The inside of the church can be divided into two parts; at the end of the first one, in the west, there is a primitive semicircular altar with frescoes of modern age; the rests of the vault and side walls are decorated with events from Vangels or Saints'lives. The frescoes, which have a liturgical as well as teaching character, are works by the artist Daniele commissioned to do it by Benedetto, an egumeno (leader of a community of monks of Greek church). Daniele, who finished the work in 1197, must be considered a local artist; in his frescoes he tried to develop Byzantine models in an original way. Through his work we can see the rise and the development of a popular and local pictorial current.

The province of Taranto

People who choose the Ionian arch included in the province of Taranto, for their historico-artistical itineraries, immediately realize the features which make it different even within a cultural homogeneity we can notice in the whole region, but above all in the properly peninsular part.

The remarkable difference among the dialects spoken along the whole arch which marks the boundary of the province of Taranto, the considerable difference of climate and of form between the places on the coast and those in the hinterland, are only some data which make present a historical differentiation which takes roots in the glorious past of Taranto, a leader town of Hellenistic "decapoli" and continuously in conflict with the native population, above all in the southern Apulia.

The province of Taranto, besides, is relatively young as it was constructed in 1923 during the Fascism and till then it was included in the province of Lecce.

But what makes Taranto even more characteristic is its condition of industrial town, the first one in Mezzogiorno (the South of Italy), whose culture, now being consolidated in more than thirty years of activity, is continuously encouraged to start processes of variety of production in order to determine again its position in consequence of the crisis of the pre-eminence of steel. As a matter of fact, the town has already consolidated this own culture which, even if it has resulted from the choice of economic politics decided by the public intervention, has deeply taken roots in its social and civil situation; so the town has developed, in political, economical and social fields, the awareness of the necessity to face firmly the challenges issued by the European integration. Taranto wants to take into consideration its happy geographical position again, which was the cause of the choices which favoured it during the centuries: from the Greeks to Napoleon, who put it in a central position in comparison with the basin of the Mediterranean, which influenced its fortunes and which, for ages, made it also "attractive" for waves of colonizers.

The history of Taranto takes its origins from the legend which presents two different tales which point out as many main characters of the foundation of the town such as: Taras, the son of Neptune, God of sea;

of Falanto, leader of Partens who probably would leave Sparta for political reasons, about the 8th century BC.

Surely Taranto was colonized by the Spartans in archaic age and it became the leading town of the peninsular Magna Graecia becoming a "megalopoli" with a population of three hundred thousand inhabitants. It allied itself with the other great Spartan colony, Syracuse for a long time, which it supported in the conflict with the Athensian fleet intervened in support of Segesta.

It was about the 5th century BC., when the town was governed by the philosopher and mathematician Archita, that the town reached the height of glorious history, for the beauty of its magnificent palaces, for the temples, for the spas and for the proverbial high way of life, witnessed by so many archaeological finds.

But very soon Taranto, which was never in good relations either with Lucans or with Messapians, began being aware of the pressure of Rome which, at first, asked for a fair conciliation pacifically, then it attacked the town after a serious offence to Roman messengers (outrage of Filonide). The intervention of Pyrrus, Epirus's king succeeded in avoiding damage, in 282, but ten years later the superiority of Rome succeeded in overwhelming Taranto. But the latter went on being hostile to Rome and, during the Punic wars, it sided with Hannibal, taking heavily the consequences: in 209 it was occupied and sacked by the legions led by Quintus Fabius Maximus, who deported to Rome 30.000 Tarantine and Carthaginiense slaves.

Taranto, which was later rehabilitated by the ruler himself, became a holiday resort and especially Horatio remembers it so. But Taranto is no longer a "megalopoli" (a very great town) like once and slowly its importance decreases till it completely integrates itself in the history of the Italian South.

The falling of the Roman Empire caused disorders in all the territories already administered by Rome. In 542 the Eternal City was occupied by the Goths led by Totila who, ten years later, was defeated by the Byzantine troops of Narsete, sent by the Emperor Justinian. Taranto was governed by the Greeks, then by the Longobards, and it was included in the duchy of Benevento. After that, it was domina-

Taranto, sunset in the Gulf

ted by the Moors who, in 927, sacked it and deported part of the population to Africa.

It was the Byzantine Emperor Niceforo Foca who rebuilt Taranto at the end of the first millennium, giving the present old town a lasting aspect, and, according to some testimonies, widening the area with artificial fill up system. Then the town was dominated by the Swabians, the Angevins and finally by the Aragoneses. These, with Ferdinand I, favoured the rebuilding of the Castle which was accomplished in 1492, after that Alfonso from Calabria had ordered to cut an isthmus in the strip of the land which separated the town from the present village.

For many years, the town, like the whole Mezzogiorno (South of Italy), was under the Spanish domination, which repressed it, killing any maritime inclination and potentialities, so at the outbreak of French Revolution, a revolutionary spirit ran through Taranto. Later on, above all with Napoleon, and then with Giuseppe Bonaparte (whose work was carried on by Gioacchino Murat), the French realized and emphasized the strategic role of the town giving it a lasting military mark and pointing out the military functions of the port. In 1865, when the princes

Umberto and Amedeo of Savoia visited the town, there was the beginning of the development of the town beyond the too narrow borders of the isle. These are important decades for its history: in 1887 the swing Bridge was inaugurated, two years later the military Arsenal too. In 1893 there was the launch of the first unit of the fleet, built in the basins of the Arsenal, the "Apulia".

In 1914 Tosi naval docks were built and, half a century later, the fourth iron Centre was opened, the latter causing, for Ionic economy, the beginning of a new age, in spite of the ups and downs influenced by the state of steel world market. Nevertheless new productive plans are concerned with steel itself and

favour above all the infrastructures of means of transportation. The improvement the town has achieved in the last decades makes us realize that other horizons can still open up in the plan of the opening of new markets.

For our journey to the province of Taranto we must go on from north-west to south-east that is from the western side on the border with Basilicata, more exactly with the province of Matera to the eastern side, in direction of the province of Lecce, so following the Ionian coast which slopes down southwards. Two sides which have some essential differences, especially because the first one is close to Murge, culminating in Martina Franca which, stretching towards the province of Bari, is in a central position, while the eastern one, which ideally begins from Taranto itself, develops on an almost completely flat territory.

Besides, the western side is characterised by the form of the territory which has historically allowed urban settlements a unitary origin, because nowadays it represents one of the most important tourist attractions: we are referring to the "gravine", ravines hollowed out by channels which take the water going down from Murge towards the sea. Along the sides of these ravines (which are in Ginosa, Laterza, Castellaneta, Mottola, Palagiano, Palagianello, Massafra, Crispiano, Statte and even Grottaglie, on the borders with the province of Brindisi) the so-called "rupestrian (rocky) civilization" has developed.

Therefore we reach the capital from Ginosa, anciently called Genusium, a small elegant town surrounded by a characteristic ravine, on whose summit rises the castle, built in Medieval age, when the whole town was fortified by the Swabians, but rebuilt by Doria family during the Renaissance.

The mother-church also belongs to the Renaissance, completed at the end of the 16th century, but it is in late Romanesque style. The two main

Ginosa's ravines are Rivolta and Casale. In both of them there are still many crypts and rupestrian (rocky) churches which have been generally preserved. In particular, in Rivolta ravine, we can still visit the crypt of St. Bartolomeo as well as the church and the crypt of St. Sofia. In Casale ravine, on the contrary, there are the rupestrian Church of Ecce Homo and the crypts of St. Domenica and St. Leonardo. In the first one which has a plan with three aisles, the frescoes of Christ Pantocrator and of the Saint which gives the name to the crypt, are in very good conditions. Ginosa, which is few kilometres far from Matera, is the small town which, for its position, is very similar to this town of Basilicata, recently considered as heritage for all the world, which can be surely the starting point of the rupestrian itinerary.

But Ginosa, a small charming town, has also an attractive suburb on the coast, Ginosa Marina, a pleasant resort where there are well-equipped tourist establishments of great glamour, above all in the famous resort of Riva of Tessali, with one of the most beautiful Italian golf-courses.

Some kilometres on towards the north-east there is Laterza, a place of the ancient prestige, linked, for customs and culture, with Matera, both of them belonging to the Land of Bari. As a matter of fact, Frederick II from Sweden, who played an important role in the fortunes of these lands, gave Laterza to the Bishops of Bari. Then it became the favourite feud of the Spaniards who established a considerable group of nobles. It was probably due to them that the town developed the pottery handicraft above all in Baroque age, imported there, as far as we know, from Campania, unfortunately disappeared in the first half of this century. Laterza also rises at the edges of a majestic ravine, studded with caves and rupestrian churches among which we must mention the important Sanctuary of Mater Domini, where there are precious rupestrian frescoes. We must point out the castle of late Medieval age and the mother church, whose front is of late Gothic style, which keeps Renaissance frescoes.

If we go on with our itinerary towards Taranto we will reach Castellaneta, a 10th century small town which, placed on a rocky spur stretching towards a ravine, played an important role in the western territory of the ancient Principality of Taranto, till it later

became an episcopal seat, the only one, besides that of Taranto, in the Ionic province.

Famous for being the birthplace of Rodolfo Valentino, to whom a monument is dedicated in the main town street, Castellaneta, the ancient Castanetum, is also the final destination of the ideal itinerary of the Baroque style in Apulia, of which the most important signs can be noticed in the cathedral dating back to the 14th century but later completely restored, above all in the late Baroque age, and in the bishop's Palace. The latter, dating back to the 17th century, keeps a wooden choir of the same age as well as the beautiful wooden polyptych, dating back to 1531, which represents Madonna with the Infant Jesus, achieved by Girolamo from Santacroce. The front of the Church of St. Caterina from Bologna also bears witness to the Baroque style. The mother-church keeps, among others, some paintings by Domenico Carella and Carlo Porta.

We must remember the basilica-crypt of St. Mary of Costantinopoli, dating back to the 9th century, among the rupestrian churches of Castellaneta, which rise on the swamps surrounding the town, and among which it is pleasant to walk in search of the human and historical traces which the archaeologists like defining "humanism of the stone".

Castellaneta also has got a suburb on the coast, Castellaneta Marina, surrounded by woods of flourishing Aleppo pines.

If we go back along the provincial road, we will see that the plain is a flourishing of blooming citrus orchards above all thanks to the fertilization which has happened, in this side of the province, after the achievement of the plans of irrigation. If we go on, we will leave behind us Palangianello, also surrounded by a ravine studded with rupestrian settlements, and dominated by the castle of Stella Caracciolo Counts.

On the top of a hill, going on towards Taranto, we can see the outline of another small beautiful town which, from a height of 390 metres, faces the plain. It is Mottola which has the charm of a hilly town with its rarefied and enchanting atmosphere, surrounded by ravines too which bear witness to important rupestrian settlements especially in the pleasant place of Casalrotto and in that of Petruscio, an important rupestrian village.

Massafra, frescoes in the ravine

Of particular importance are the rupestrian churches which are so many and generally preserved and with a considerable plan. Among these: St. Angelo in Casalrotto, dating back to 13th century, with three aisles. The rupestrian church of St. Gregorio, placed in the homonymous ravine, has also three aisles and keeps a Byzantine fresco of Christ Pantocrator; opposite to it rises the church of the Madonna of Seven Lamps with two apsidal aisles.

The hill of Mottola, placed on a particularly happy and strategic position, in the ramifications of Murge which slope down to the plane of Taranto,

hosted settlements since the Hellenistic age and on several occasions during the Middle Ages, till it passed to Caracciolo family, in the half of the 17th century.

A monument which is worthy of attention is surely the mother-Church, achieved in the 16th century on a plan of Norman age and whose particular front is in Venetian style. The bell tower of the same age is precious, but it shows a superimposition of different styles.

Let's go down the plane and leave the pastures and the breedings of Murgia which produce delicious milk, rich in milk casein (that's why it is considered of

Massafra, the Castle

higher quality), and "plane down" among the fruitful orange-groves of Palagiano and its Conca d'Oro facing the Gulf of Taranto. And here we will leave behind us the beaches of Chiatona too in order to take again the itinerary of the Appian Way and reach Massafra (32.000 inhabitants). It is a small extraordinary town with an unusual form, being clearly divided into two halves, either horizontally or vertically, by the ravine of St. Marco, which runs through it completely. At the foot of the ravine lies the old village (called Land). On its top, the new suburb (Borgo Santa Caterina) stands out, developed towards north-east,

on the both sides of the gorge sloping down to the old village. The gorge is dominated by two bridges, the first of which is a majestic old stone bridge which unites the two big rocks, allowing the elegant Corso Italia , beginning from the very central Vittorio Emanuele Square, to reach Garibaldi Square.

Besides being the fourth Commune, for the number of its inhabitants, among the 29 of the province of Taranto, and for its suggestive beauty of its views, we must point out Massafra because it is the small town which keeps the highest number of rupestrian churches and crypts of basilian (referring to St. Basilio and

The Ionian coastline

his believers) age in the whole Apulia, among which we find the Church of the Madonna della Buona Nuova and the Crypt of Candelora with three aisles and valuable frescoes.

The Sanctuary of the Madonna della Scala, destination for pilgrimages is worthy of a particular mention, it is at the bottom of the homonymous ravine, a pleasant and suggestive place which is surely worthy of a careful visit.

The castle offers a really particular sight, stretching in the ravine of St. Marco with the octagonal tower, the biggest of the four ones which surrounds the square building. Built in the 14th century on the foundations of a pre-existing fortification, probably built by the Normans, now it belongs to the Commune of Massafra. The first structure of the mother Church dates back to the 15th century, but we must point out above all the presence of Baroque art: beginning from the chapel of St. Lorenzo in the same church and from the front of the convent of St. Agostino, on the Appian state road. Other Baroque monuments are the Tower of the clock belonging to the beginning of the 18th century, and the Church of St. Benedetto belonging to some years before.

Taranto

The rural landscape which surrounds the built-up area in the north, either towards Mottola, or towards Crispiano is delightful, on whose way we find some examples of typical farmhouses, especially towards Martina Franca, along whose provincial road we find the delightful wood of Pianelle which seems to us a place suitable for the fairy tales of our early childhood.

We can take the way again to approach Taranto, going on along the Appian state road. Here we find the majestic chimneys of the Fourth Iron Centre which signal us the approach to the industrial area of the capital. On left the Ilva plant, the greatest industrial works in Europe, stretches for many kilometres. On right other plants: Belleli, the biggest in the Mediterranean with the oil platforms intended for all the seas in the world; the Cementir and Agip oil-refinery. So we arrive at the industrial capital of the South, from Croce quarter which, through a sharp bridge, leads us to the old part of the town.

Taras, the mythical son of Neptun was really shrewd as, according to the legend, he chose Taranto as his landing-point about 4.000 years ago. The land on which the two smooth and fishy seas lap must have seemed to him a wonderful land favoured by Gods. The strip of land which separates the two seas,

Taranto, the Castle

during the centuries, has always seemed a "safe", lucky and attractive spot.

The peninsula, a real isle after the cutting of the navigable channel, was the heart of Taranto till some decades ago, when the first collapses obliged thousands of people from Taranto "to go into exile" and when the restoration plan of the town began to be put into action whose results can be seen, even if they are below the expectations, for the inadequacy of available public funds.

After the disappearance, in the western part of the isle, of the scaffolds after years of laborious restores, whose plans were accepted unanimously by all over the world, the original aspect of the ancient structures has come out of layers of lime, even if unfortunately collapses and transennae can still be seen.

Looking at the East, we will leave behind us, on the headland separated from the isle, by the stone bridge, the industrial area, value and defect of the present Taranto. Turning left, soon we will reach the "Marina", the inside promenade facing the Small Sea (which, for a long way, in front of us, barracks and naval docks face) along which the wholesale and retail trade of fish takes place, and to whose banks the boats and the fishing boats are moored, far from the billows of the sea. We can breathe the good smell of

the isle, through the alleys, where we must walk in Indian file, we find the promenade Vittorio Emanuele II, commonly known as the "ringhiera" (railing). Here the view changes: a higher level separates from the sea, while, before, the horizon becomes larger; the strips of land extend and stretch along the beautiful Cheradi isles including the Big Sea which hosts the mercantile port on the right bank.

In the Medieval Borgo (suburb) stands out the Church of St. Domenico Maggiore, built in the 14th century (while according to the tradition it is dated back to Frederick II who had probably his palace there) on the ancient Byzantine structure of St. Pietro Imperiale with the beautiful staircase which was added in Baroque age.

If we follow the "ringhiera" (railing), we will find Amati Palace, seat of university institutions and schools for special aims as to the sea, we will reach the Cathedral of St. Cataldo, among luxury palaces, to which the archbishopric is annexed. Brought back to its original Romanesque style through recent restores, the Cathedral Basilica dates back to 1071, but it was often changed. The front is in Baroque style, the plan with three aisles, by Mauro Manieri (1713), is supported by columns of different styles and ages (from Corinthian to Palaeochristian, completely originating from ancient structures). But the most valuable artistic example is represented by the baroque "cappellone" (big chapel) devoted to St. Cataldo patron, a "jewel box" with wonderful inlays achieved through the marble got out of the archaeological finds which once were spread throughout the territory of the town. Ordered to be built by the archbishop Tommaso Caracciolo of the princes of Avellino, it was made by the most famous marble-workers of the age, among whom we find Fanzago from Naples and Lombardelli from Carrara to whom the wonderful frontal is attributed. The frescoes of the vault (1713) are by De Matteis. Interesting is the crypt which shows

the sea, whose waters, though surrounded as they were a salt lake, don't stagnate above all thanks to many litres of fresh water which overflow from the crust of the underwater world.

A few steps inside and we will find ourselves in the heart of the restored area. The itinerary among the monumental inhabited areas which have been brought to light begins from the characteristic Cava street, a central point of the old part which has revived as a suggestive stage of a restored age.

On the opposite side, after shortly going through

Big chapel of St. Cataldo

Byzantine frescoes, some of which have been recently restored.

If we follow Cathedral street, where we find old monastic buildings (St. Chiara and St. Francesco from Assisi) and noble palaces (such as the restored Galeota palace) intended to host important and social structures, we will reach Castle Square. And here the perspectives change again, the horizons become larger, showing from one side the columns of the Doric temple, one of the rare significant witnesses of the past of Magna Graecia, and the Town Hall, in front of it the Aragonese castle, an imposing defensive struc-ture, widened and rebuilt by Ferdinando I from Aragon in 1492 and recently seat of organizations of the Navy, but also of the two most beautiful town galleries, the first being managed by the Commune, the second one by the Navy itself.

The swing Bridge, unique "physical contact" between the isle and the "new town" is almost the symbol of Taranto. For over a century (exactly since 1887, even it has been built more times) it has joined the two suburbs, the ancient and the modern one, passing the navigable channel, through which the naval units which reach the arsenal of the Navy or the naval buildings enter the roadstead of the Small Sea.

The promenade with trees, looking on to the Great Sea, has always been the pride of Taranto: its beauty, the sight it shows in every hour of the day, are worthy of attention which any tourist always pays. Its flourishing palm-trees, the walk there able to make our minds wander far from the noise of the town, are always a button-hole flower for Taranto. On that promenade, where in "the fabulous sixties" it was used to film scenes about mariners, nowadays the lovers, above all soldiers still meet.

On the other side of the swing bridge, the one which faces the Small Sea, the view is perhaps even more suggestive, though limited by military installations.

From Rome street the eye roves beyond the bridge, succeeding in seeing from afar the outline of Murge of Martina Franca. From Rome street we can reach the thalassographic Institute of Cnr, an ancient scientific structure, endowed with modern systems for oceanographic and bacteriological researches.

A few steps forward and we will reach the gardens of "Peripato", an ancient and delightful villa, already annexed to the 15th century convent of St. Anthony, nowadays under repair. At a short distance, in Corso (Main street) Umberto , there is the national Museum of Magna Graecia, placed in the ex-convent of Alcantarini. Established over one hundred years ago, the Museum now under a rebuilding plan also concerning the transfer of the archaeological superintendence which has been recently annexed, to the old town, is very important for the archaeology of Magna Graecia as it offers over 6.000 finds among which there are the valuable and charming jewels of Hellenistic age recently admired throughout the world, but it keeps in its cellars, over 100.000.

The other important cultural structure of the town is Acclavio Library which keeps in the two seats where it is placed, the palace of government, an imposing structure built during the Fascism, and Umberto's palace of offices, the most meaningful architectural structure in Borgo, works of great historico-cultural value such as: incunabula, manuscripts and cinquecentine (books dating back to the 16th century).

In front of us there is the Borgo with D'Aquino street, above all a meeting point for people living in Taranto. From here the present Taranto begins, which, thanks to the boom of steal, has frenetically extended, even irrationally sometimes making the area larger and creating new outskirts. As a symbol of need of new aims, able to give its quarters a more modern and rational aspect, the great bridge Punta Penna Pizzone, recently dedicated to Aldo Moro stands out on the inside bank of the Small Sea in order to separate the two inlets; a bridge which, with its 1.250 metres in height, has given the town not only a means of communication for entrance and exit traffic, but also an incomparable view.

Among the modern structures, stands out, in the new town, the famous Cathedral Gran Madre di Dio (Great Mother of God), planned in the seventies by the great architect Gio Ponti from Milan. Imagined as a great white sail rising towards the sky and rich in symbols relating to the sea, the cathedral, one of the most important examples in Neo-gothic style, rises at the join between Viale (Avenue) Magna Graecia and the very long Dante street.

Nevertheless, a short walk around the town, will show us many important historical witnesses, beginning from the Aqueduct of Triglio, for the most part preserved, dating back to the late Medieval age, but on a plan which could even date back to Hellenistic age, whose arcades are along the road for Statte, to reach, towards north-west, the Abbey of St. Mary of Justice, the only Gothic-planned structure in the town, which was a fixed way for Crusaders going to the Holy Land.

A fairyland. So the Valley of Itria shows the visitors, with its multicoloured handkerchiefs (pieces) of land, embroidered on a variegated and "capricious" (unpredictable) ground, surrounded by small party walls, which cut off the sharp colours of land, vineyards and trees, and above all of the white-grey colours of trulli, enchanting, absurd, unrepeatable rural types of architecture.

We are in Martina Franca (46.000 inhabitants), the "roof" of the province of Taranto, with its 500 metres in height, on the borders with the provinces of Bari and Brindisi. Our itinerary for the eastern side of the province begins from here. The sight in its valley is unique: in a variety of bright and contrasting colours stand out the trulli, or "casedde" as they are com-

Martina Franca, the church of St. Domenico

monly called: ancient houses whose origins date back to previous age, perhaps to the prehistory. They represent a bright architectural intuition as they are able to grant a shelter from different climates either when it is very hot in summer or when the snow often covers these areas in winter.

But Martina Franca, the town which was established in the 14th century by Philip d'Angiò, Prince of Taranto on a previous settlement of Tarantines who found shelter in those lands around the 10th century, which became feud of Caracciolo family in 1507 and now is also the capital of Baroque in relation with the province of Taranto. It has been worthy, for its uniqueness and beauty, of the attention of qualified scholars who have pointed out that the Baroque theme which permeates all the wide old part of the town, represents a singular feature both for the stylistics connotations and for the gracefulness of forms.

Caracciolo family surely gave a sharp mark for the beginning of such singular flourishing as they favoured the building of Ducal Palace in 1668 on the ruins of the ancient castle. The plan, which, according to tradition, was supposed to be realized through a plan by Bernini (nevertheless it seems that he was asked only a stylistic opinion) must be attributed to Giovanni Andrea Larducci. In the great rooms of the famous house, which today hosts the Town Hall, stands out the great frescoed pictorial scenes by Domenico Carella from Martina.

A masterpiece of the so-called "Salentine Baroque" is the collegiate Church of St. Martino (1737) with its magnificent porch, its marbles and its silver statues of St. Nicola and St. Comasia.

Famous Baroque monuments are represented by the churches of St. Domenico, Madonna del Carmine, St. Francesco. Among many remarkable palaces we must mention: the Caroli, Fanelli, Maggi, Motolese, Ancona ones. A walk in the old part of the town will reveal among the suggestive alleys, small masterpie-ces at every corner.

Let's go down the coastal road of Orimini which makes Murge slope down towards south-east to reach Grottaglie (32.000 inhabitants), Apulia's capital of pottery, one of the nineteen Italian places of ancient and famous artisan tradition recognized by law.

But let's make a detour of few kilometres to reach Crispiano (13.000 inhabitants), a small beautiful town surrounded by caves hollowed out by tufaceous stone, where suggestive performances take place during the year such as: the living crib. Among its other monuments we must signal the abbey Crypt of St. Mary of Crispiano which keeps frescoes of

Byzantine age, representing the Virgin, St. Nicola and St. Michele.

That form which changes under the skill hands of the craftsman has something magic. The wet land lets it be dominated, moulded following the movement of an ancient dance. It rises from the lathe, shaping itself in different and unrepeatable forms, like the gestures of an artist who creates. We have arrived at Grottaglie, after leaving behind us Montemesola. After stopping the turning of the lathe here the amphora, the vase, the plate appear, shaped according to a very ancient tradition. If we see them appearing

suddenly, these "objects", authentic works of art, will awaken astonishment, interest, charm. And the creative gesture repeats itself endlessly, in the ancient artisan shops, hollowed out, four or five centuries ago, in tufaceous stone in the ancient ravine of Casal Piccolo, now known as the quarter of Pottery, commonly called "Camenn'ri", built at the foot of the Medieval castle.

The small town, risen in the 10th century around the first built-up areas represented by many ravines which studs the territory (among which we mention those of Riggio, Fullonese, Buccito, Pensieri) was assigned to the bishop's palace of Taranto by Roberto il Guiscardo and, after alternate events, it passed again to the latter in the 16th century. The castle will be always bishop's palace even under the jurisdiction of the princes and feudatories who will follow one another till the 18th century.

Handicraft takes roots in the age of Magna Graecia. Objects of precious making, achieved in many settlements risen around Taranto, are kept in the national Museum, and surely between the 15th and the 16th centuries some places of our province reached the flourishing of handicraft. The pottery production of Grottaglie can be divided into two currents. The "ruagnara" art and the "faenzara" art. The first one comprehends common objects, generally "ingobbiati", that is dipped in hot clay, or glazed with lead-bearing glazes. Through the "faenzara" art we define the tin-glazed pottery, more finely worked, for a more decorative use.

The under repair episcopal palace, and the 16th century garden represent the summit of the ancient Borgo, in whose heart, with its front in the beautiful Queen Margherita square, there is the mother-Church which includes inside the beautiful Baroque "cappellone" devoted to St. Ciro. Near there we find the sanctuary devoted to St. Francesco De Geronimo, the only Saint of the province of Taranto.

Other precious monuments are: the Crib by Stefano from Putignano of 1530, kept in the Church del Carmine, annexed to the majestic monastic building, and the Church of St. Francesco of Paola with the beautiful completely frescoed cloister (like that of Carmine too).

From Grottaglie we can easily reach some other villages of the Ionic hinterland, which still keep the traces of the past such as Carosino, with the elegant castle of D'Ayala Valva family, feudatories of Spanish origins who also ordered the luxury palaces of Monteparano, Roccaforzata and St. Giorgio to be built.

We are already in the heart of the land which was populated, in the second half of the 15th century, by the Albanians. Clear linguistic traces of this colonization can be noticed in San Marzano di San Giuseppe, whose old people are still used to speak Albanian. In its area we find the sanctuary of the Madonna of Graces, a Byzantine crypt where the Virgin is kept and worshipped in a fresco of rare beauty.

We are in the provincial road for Manduria (35.000 inhabitants), the second village of the province for its wideness. We reach here after passing through Sava (17.000 inhabitants), a small agricultural town which keeps a beautiful castle of the 16th century.

Now the landscape has completely changed. There are no hills featured by gorges and rupestrian settlements: boundless planes with luxuriant vegetation and wide and famous vineyards open before us.

Manduria, a small elegant town of very ancient origins offers a glorious past: one of the most important town of Messapian Decapoli, fortified and protected with strong megalithic walls, of which important traces can still be seen.

The town-walls which have been brought to light during the excavations are three, of which the most ancient, that is the innermost one, is supposed to date back to the age between the 5th and 4th centuries BC.

The ancient Manduria, stronghold of Messapians, was separated from Taranto by great rivalries and, in spite of the huge power of the leading town of Decapoli, it succeeded in holding out against its continuous assaults. On the contrary, it was Rome, for the first time, to join its lands to it, which then followed the ups and downs of the Roman Empire, ending by falling into Totila's hands, who destroyed the small town in 547. In 977 it was destroyed by the Saracens and then around 1090 it was rebuilt by the Normans. In 1789 Ferdinando I of Borboun gave back it its name which had been changed into Castalnuovo by the Normans.

The town suburb, completely characterized by a

But the monument of much more importance and suggestion is surely represented by Plinian Spring which takes its name from the quotation which Pliny the Elder made in its "Natural History" with the name of "Lacus Manduriae", but called "Scegnu" by people from Manduria. Pliny talked about a miracle referring to the fact that the water was always on the same level in the basin. The basin or spring is in the middle of a wide underground (partly artificial) cave and we can reach there through a wide staircase.

From Manduria, which represents the centre of the eastern side of the Ionian province, we can easily reach other places which, in spite of its smaller dimensions, also keep important traces of the past and where we will find surely the feudal castle such as: in Avetrana (9.000 inhabitants), on the border with the province of Lecce, which was an important feudal town and still keeps the 14th century castle and in Torricella (4.500 inhabitants) with its five tower castle of the 15th century which is one of the most beautiful castles in the area.

We are at some kilometres from the beautiful Salentine coast, which reach Capo San Vito. The beaches are long and sandy, the water is clear. The whole coast, like the Ionian one, is studded with coastal towers, built in the 16th century to prevent the territory from the assaults of the Saracen pirates, a real plague of the Southern Italy and, in particular, of the peninsulas of Apulia and Calabria. We point out, going up to Taranto: Torre (Tower) Colimena , one of the best preserved, in the homonymous spot, less than twenty kilometres from Taranto which must be also remembered for the important archaeological settlements which we find there: as a matter of fact, Saturo still keeps many traces of the Greeks who considered it one of their landing points in archaic age.

simple and elegant Baroque, offers many witnesses such as: Imperiali palace, built in 1717, by the architect Mauro Manieri, on the ruins of a Norman castle. Even the Monastery of Servite with the adjoining church is attributed to Manieri. But there also many churches being worthy of attention beginning from the Collegiate church with its very beautiful apse to the church of St. Francesco from Assisi and that of Rosario. The Cathedral, devoted to St. Gregorio is supposed to date back to Norman Age; the font of 1534 is worthy of particular attention.

The province of Lecce

Extreme ramification of Apulia, the province of Lecce, for its natural and historico-artistical goods, can host, as it is occurring, millions of tourists.

In the past Salento included not only the province of Lecce, but also the neighbouring provinces of Brindisi and Taranto. Since 1927 it has taken the present aspect and it comprehends almost one hunderds communes, each of which is rich in events and monuments of different ages and civilizations.

We propose our reader a short and simple itinerary which, beginning from Lecce, will follow an easy way. If he/she has the map ready, he/she will be able to find his/her bearings among places and stages, making, at the same time, many excursions along the way.

Of Messapian origin, Lecce, according to tradition, must have been founded in the 5th century BC. by Malennio, whose daughter Euippa married Idomeneo, the hero coming from Troia who had already defeated his father-in-law, taking possession of the reign. The town must have been originally called Sybaris, then because of Idomeneo, Lytium or Lycium. Lecce kept being a Messapian town, though it was also influenced by Magna Graecia, even after the Roman Conquest (267 BC.). It opposed the expansionistic aims of Taranto, it allied itself with Athens in the 341 year of Rome and it sent 1500 archers in support of the Greek town for the war in Sicily.

Of the mysterious Messapian people, proud of their civilization and their military power which gave a lot of trouble at first to the Magno-Greeks and then to the Romans, imposing walls, archaeological stations (Rudiae, Cavallino, Muro Leccese, Alezio, Ugento) remain in Salento and, in Lecce itself, during fortuitous excavations, sometimes appear tombs, inscriptions, funeral equipment of which we can see some finds in the local museum "S. Castromediano" while the most part of funeral furnishings is preserved in the National Museum of Taranto.

Between 629 and 267 BC., owing to the wars between the Messapian-Salentine confederates, Taranto and Pirro and the Urbe (Rome), the Roman conquest occured in Salento, where the Messapian language and the different dialects from Magna Graecia were spoken, but which, during the seven years of Latin domination, completely disappeared.

In the neighbourhood of Lecce, in the meantime declared "Statio Militum Lupiae", Quinto Ennio was born in Rudiae in 239 BC., a famous Roman poet, proud of his Roman citizenship, but also proud of his Messapian-Rudian origins.

Lecce and Salento, after occasional rebellions, linked their fortunes to Rome, to which they were always faithful and the town, taking part in Camilla tribe, also succeeded in opposing Hannibal who wasn't able to violate its walls. Roman soldiers and colonies settled in Lecce, and in particular we must remember that in 102 BC. a colony was founded, led by C. Mario Nepote and by L. Lutazio Catulo. Another colony was established in the town in 75 AD., under the power of Vespasian. Of the Roman age some epigraphs, some ruins, an amphitheatre and a theatre remain in Lecce, belonging the two last ones to the 2nd century AD.

Of Roman Age is the column which bears the statue of St. Oronzo, patron of the town, who, together with Saints Giusto and Fortunato is celebrated from 24th to 26th August. Such column, in the homonymous St. Oronzo square, is one of the two final shafts of the Appian Way, ending in Brindisi. And the people from Brindisi themselves, in the late 17th century, due to favours received by St. Oronzo, gave the column as a gift to Lecce in order to put the statue of the Saint thaumaturge on its top.

The Romans achieved the port of St. Cataldo, a famous beach for Lecce's people now, which is about 10 kilometres far from the town. Once this landing place, belonging to the Adrian age (it was so called Adrian), was one of the most important in the Adriatic, but it declined inexorably in the Middle Ages.

We can already notice the presence of Christianity in the 2nd century AD. in Lecce, which was one of the most ancient episcopal seats. Owing to the crisis of the Roman Empire the town lost its self-confidence, it suffered devastation from pirates. In 542, during the Greek-Gothic war, it was destroyed by Totila, then the Saracens arrived between the 9th and 10th centuries. On the Western Empire's falling, Lecce and a large part of Apulia became Byzantine. The town declined, it was involved in the conflicts between Byzantium and the Longobards of the grand duchy of Benevento, and Romualdo's mercenary troops conquered it in 680, granting people, after some time, piece and prosperity.

A few years later, the town was destroyed by the

Lecce, the Amphitheatre, the Sedile and the church of St. Marco

Saracens, then by the Hungarians, after that by the Slavs. The greedy Byzantine power came back and between the 8th and 9th centuries they excited the iconoclastic persecutions which obliged the monks coming from Sicily, Calabria and from the other Adriatic bank to hide themselves in the gorges of desert and woody areas and they sheltered in the hypogeal (underground) crypts they frescoed with the images of the saints of the oriental rite.

In the 10th century Otto II from Saxony subjected Lecce, which in 983 passed again to the Byzantines and it was annexed to the Catapanato of Bari. Between 1055 and 1069 the Norman conquest of Terra d'Otranto happened and Lecce became the earldom of d'Altavilla family. After saving himself from a shipwreck, in 1182 the count Tancred founded the Romanesque church of the Saints Niccolò and Cataldo (now in the cemetery), but the small contemporary church of St. Mary d'Aurìo, five kilometres far from the town is Norman too. In spite of some civil wars, under the domination of the Northern lords, Lecce was rich and powerful, in the reign it was second only to Palermo. The Normans also built mighty walls, the Mastio, now included in Carlo V's castle, the still active Benedictine Monastery of St. John the Evangelist.

After being passed to the Swabians because of the marriage between Constance d'Altavilla and Henry VI of Hohenstaufen dinasty, who procreated Frederick II, the town belonged to the Angevins in 1268 who granted it to the Brienne family as a feud,

del Balzo, princes of Taranto; 17 years later it was confiscated by the Aragonese monarchy, but it remained without any prince till the age of Carlo VIII from France who, while staying in Naples, assigned it to Gilberto of Brunswick. After that, the kings of the two Sicilies gave their third-born sons the earldom of Lecce, though as only an honourific title...

In 1480 Otranto was sacked and Lecce repelled a sally from Islamites. The following year, due to the plague, 15.000 people died, almost the same number of inhabitants who had died due to the epidemic which raged between 1466 and 1468. Flourishing Venetian, Tuscanian, Greek-Albanian, Ragusan, Hebrew and Genoese colonies had already settled in the town, trade prospered, but they were not idyllic times. During the Franco-Spanish war, Lecce in 1502 fell into transalpine people's hands and in the times of the king of Spain Ferdinand the Catholic, there was the massacre of the Hebrews who, in spite of some discrimination, had been defended by Mary of Enghien and Ferrante of Aragon.

During the Spanish power, the capital of Salento, like the other places dominated by the Iberians, was subjected to fiscal pressure. But in this period, the reminiscence of Otranto's slaughter was still alive, so the fear of the Turks lay heavy more than ever among the population of Salento. The coasts and the farmhouses were fortified, the towns were surrounded by walls and Lecce was also endowed with new defensive buildings. In 1539 Carlo V ordered to build new town-walls and a mighty castle which, planned by Gian Giacomo dell'Acaya, still today rises proud, while of the fortified walls with ramparts only few parts in bad conditions remain. In the meantime the Medieval town was disappearing and Lecce was fortified by Ferrante Loffredo, master of Terra d'Otranto, according to the criteria required by the use of artil-

then in 1356 it belonged to the Enghien family, under whose power it was favoured, above all in the times of the countess Mary who married Raimondello Orsini del Balzo in 1385 and, remaining a widow, she became the wife of King Ladislao who married her only for political aims. The 14th century tower of Belloluogo (nice place), on the old road for Surbo dates back to the age of Brienne family. Together with the tower of Parco, built in the 15th century by Giovannantonio del Balzo, heir to Mary, it represents a symbolic witness of the Angevin military architecture, before the use of fire-arms.

In 1446 Lecce was under the domination of Orsini

Lecce, Celestines palace and Santa Croce

lery. When Lecce became the capital of Apulia (1539) it extended its borders, it took a more rational aspect, it adorned itself with churches, convents, palaces, administrative and judicial organs, it became an attractive place for nobles, artists and men of letters.

Sciences and arts flourished, various academies were built such as: Lupiense (15th century), that of Trasformati (16th century), of Speculatori (18th century) and finally Salentine Academy, later founded by Jesuite Fathers.

In the 16th century Lecce finally lived in piece, a piece guarded by numerous and powerful clergy who favoured brotherhoods, congregations, and schools which managed efficient spiritual centres. Thanks to the church, charitable and philanthropic institutions were built in order to relieve the miseries of the poor and foundlings. The town had remained out of the storm of the Protestant Reform, and only with the presence of Theatines and Jesuites, respectively arrived in 1574 and 1586, it lived the new spirit of the Church renewed by the Council of Trent.

Between the 16th and 17th centuries a feverish atmosphere pervaded the town which became a huge central point for so many civil and religious works that private people, ecclesiastic congregations and secular clergy busied themselves raising again and

Lecce, the Cathedral and the Bishop's palace

again beautiful, imposing, buildings in a sort of constant emulation which gave shape to the present aspect of the old part of Lecce, where we can notice the triumph of Baroque everywhere.

Nevertheless it is a particular and unrepeatable Baroque, influenced by the theatrical and spectacular taste of the Spanish culture, but it is made unique by the characteristics of the local stone, ductile, ready for any engraving, any arabesque, being of a straw colour which also generates heat. There were many skilled workers of "leccìsu", sculptors and stone cutters who embellished the fronts and altars and the insides of patrician houses and of middle class who, in their turn, emulated the mighty ones for wealth.

Among the most famous monuments of this age we must remember the Arch of Triumph, built in 1548 in honour of Charles V and, among so many churches the first of all is the basilica of Santa Croce (Cross), built between 1549 and 1646 with the adjoining Convent of Celestines, today seat of the Provincial administration and Prefecture. For this church, which represents the highest and the most accomplished expression of the Baroque in Lecce, famous local architects such as: G. Riccardi, C. Penna and G. Zimbalo as well as engravers and stone-cutters lavish their own talents. We can notice the triumph of Baroque above all in the front of the temple, a front rich in symbols, statues, decorations and allegories.

The "church-town" has got a famous Cathedral, in a suggestive and homonymous square, where we also find the Bishop's Palace and the Seminary. Built in 1114 and completely rebuilt between 1659 and 1670

Lecce, the small well in the Seminary and the altar of the Crucified in the church of Rosario

by Giuseppe Zimbalo, the author of the imposing bell tower too, this temple devoted to the Virgin Mary has got Baroque altars, the crib by G. Riccardi and the crypt of 1517.

In G. Libertini street we find the churches of St. John the Baptist (or of Rosario) of 17th century, of St. Ann (17th century) and St. Teresa (17th century). On Corso Vittorio Emanuele rises the temple of St. Irene, built between 16th and 17th centuries, according to a plan by F. Grimaldi, with a front in Cinquecento style. In St. Oronzo square, few metres far from the column of the Patron of the town, there are the ex small church of St. Marco and the Sedile, both of them of the 16th century. In front of the Roman amphitheatre, still partly buried, we find the church of Santa Maria della Grazia (of Grace), built at the end of the 16th century,

with classical influences, planned by F. Coluzio. Near there, in Maremonti street there is the church of St. Anthony from Padua (or of St. Joseph), of 1566, but with front and inside restorations of the 18th century. At a short distance, in Vittorio Emanuele II square we find the church of St. Chiara, probably raised in 1694 by G. Cino. In Perroni street, the church of St. Matteo is not so far, built by A. Larducci between 1667 and 1700, with the characteristic front which reminds us of that of the temple of San Carlo alle Quattro Fontane (St. Charles to the Four Fountains), in Rome. In Rubichi street we find the church of Jesus or del Buon consiglio (of the Good advice), raised by the Jesuites in the late 16th century and planned by G. de Rosis; in the small square of SS. Addolorata (Our Lady of Sorrows) we find the church of St. Angel, probably built G. Zimbalo, in 1663. Near there, in Peruzzi square, the church of St. Mary of Angels (or of San Francesco di Paola) of the 16th century and finally, in Tancred square, the church of Carmine, rebuilt from 1711 to 1717 by G. Cino, on a 16th century building.

These are Lecce's churches, but the tourist can still find out so many ones and wandering for the town he/she can observe the superb noble palaces which, between the 16th century and the 18th century, brought prestige and honour to the old part of the town. Among the 16th century buildings we must remember the following palaces: Vernazza-Castromediano, Guarini, Gorgoni, Loffredo-Adorni, Saraceno, Martirano, Pensini-Morisco, Fumarola-Spada, Perrone, Panzera, Prato, della Ratta, Giaconìa, Prioli, Giustiniani, de Raho, Morelli, Maresgallo, Luperto, Lecciso, Zimara, Forleo and Mettola. The following palaces are in Seicento style: Costantini, Lanzialao, Tafuri, Personè, Paladini, Giugni, Grassi-Cattani, Rossi, Mariscalchi, Martucci, and Palumbo. Of the 18th century, then, are the palaces such as: Marrese, Guarini, Balsamo, Belli, Palumbo, Rollo, de Simone, Manieri, Montefusco, D'Amore, Lopez y Royo-Personè, Tresca, Carrozzo, Stabile, Bozzicorso, Lubelli and Tiso.

The history of Lecce, during the 16th century, was without any important events, but the 17th century was not surely quiet. The news of the revolt of Masaniello, in Naples (1647) spread over the town, nevertheless every attempt of rebellion was severely repressed. The Spanish misrule squeezed population very much, besides there were also the abuses of greedy feudatories, civil wars broke out in the town for political factions too so that in 1646 the bishop Pappacoda was obliged to arm all the clergy.

The town of Lecce is not only famous for its churches and its Baroque palaces, but also for a very typical art which, though achieved through poor material, has produced and still produces, though in a minor tone, works of undisputed value and prestige. We are referring to the paper-pulp, already used in the 17th century, which has slowly seen the flourishing of famous artists such as: Pietro Surgente ("mesciu Pietru de li Cristi"), Achille de Lucrezi, Giovanni Andrea De Pascalis, Luigi Guacci, Giuseppe Manzo, Raffaele Carretta, Antonio Malecore, Pitro Indino and Angelo Capoccia, who have illustrated so many churches of Lecce, in Italy and in the world, with their paper Saints and with their "shepherds", which still today show themselves during the "Fair of St. Lucia" (13th-14th December), when "pupi" (small paper puppets which represent the characters of the Nativity) and cribs are exhibited.

An awful plague afflicted Lecce in 1656, and St. Oronzo was supposed to have stopped the plague, since then the Saint protomartyr has become the Patron of the town.

In the 18th century, a prolific year for letters and arts, churches and palaces kept being built. But the town life was sad as it was subjected to the rigours of ecclesiastical collectors of taxes. In 1710 a revolt broke out against the clergy, the king supported the population which was excommunicated by the bishop Fabrizio Pignatelli, whose interdict lasted till 1719. The abuses of power committed by the nobles and the town conflicts tormented the population.

In 1749 the Hebrews were definitely expelled from Lecce, by order of Charles III of Borboun.

The Enlightenment, in 1799, ended in the Parthenopean reign with the famous revolutionary riots which exalted republic. In Lecce too, on 9th February of that year the tree of freedom was raised, but after 24 hours it was cut down and then there was the cruel repression on the part of the reactionary clergy and royalists. After two centuries of subjection to Bourbons, in 1821 Lecce took part in the rebellion of the liberals who 27 years later set up a provisional government. The Risorgimento in Lecce includes, among the other ones, famous characters such as: Giuseppe Libertini and Sigismondo Castromediano. Finally, in 1860, the town was annexed to the Reign of Italy and, after the Unity, between 1895 and 1915, for the first time it extended beyond the 16th century walls, endowing itself with many public buildings.

In this period the walls fortified with rampart were demolished and their ruins were used to fill up the ditches of putrid and miasmatic water. In these rooms, above all along viale (Avenue) Gallipoli and viale Lo Re, some small villas of eclectic style were slowly built, constructions which show something exotic, oriental which harmonizes with the trends of time and with building and decorative experiences already present in the town, the neo-classical ones, together with the most various styles.

Lecce, the front of Santa Croce

In the north of Lecce we find Campi Salentina which, inhabited since the Bronze Age, around 924 AD. hosted the refugees of the hamlets of Bagnara, Firmigliano, Afra and Ainoli, destroyed by the Saracens. Campi rised in that way, where Frederick II built a castle, restored in the 16th century and completely transformed into Baroque forms in 1627.

Very interesting is the parish church of the Madonna of Grazie (Graces) (16th century) of Renaissance forms which harmonize with the Baroque. The inside, completed in the 18th century, keeps carved wooden works, good ancient paintings and the Renaissance monument to Bellisario Maramonte. In the neighbouring countryside there is the dilapidated Romanesque church of St. Mary dell'Alto.

Not so far from Campi is Squinzano. Famous agricultural centre, Squinzano has got the parish church of St. Nicola of 1612, but of Renaissance style, the contemporary church of Calvario and the church of Annunziata. At 7 kilometres from the village, towards north-east, we find the Abbey of St. Mary of Cerrate (12th century), made up of the Romanesque church with the beautiful portal and of the ancient coenobium, later transformed into a farmhouse. The structure, restored after years of unjust abandon, hosts the Museum of Arts and Popular Traditions of Salento.

The church, with three aisles and three apses, still has got frescoes of 13th, 15th and 16th centuries. The front with only a cusp has a central rose window, small decorative arches, the porch, with a protiro (an arch supported by two columns on the porch), sculptured with scenes from Nativity. On the left side we find the elegant portico supported by small columns with figure capitals.

If we leave Squinzano and pass through Trepuzzi we will reach Novoli, where a human settlement has been documented since the Bronze Age, but Novoli was already inhabited in the Middle Ages around a basilian "grancia" (a convent with an annexed farmhouse). Then arrived here the inhabitants of Porziano, a marshy hamlet which was abandoned as it was unhealthy. Starting from the 11th century the place was called St. Mary la Nuova, then Novole and, in the 18th century, Novoli.

Interesting is the 18th century parish church, with emphasized Baroque reminiscences, devoted to St. Andrea the Apostle. The sanctuary of St. Anthony the Abbot is very refined, with the Madonna of Bread, the former being Patron of the village where, on 16th January, for the celebrations in honour of the saint hermit, a huge and famous bonfire (fòcara) is made gathering so many people from the area of Salento. It is worth visiting the neo-Gothic and the convent of Passionist Fathers, the small church of the Immaculate endowed with Byzantine frescoes, the four-sided

Roca

castle achieved in the 16th century.

Some kilometres from the South of Lecce we will find Cavallino, important archaeological station of Messapian origin, which has got the fortified palace in Cinquecento style, belonging to Castromediano family (15th-16th centuries) and changed during the time. This monument is endowed with a precious but simple crenellated front and a portico (loggia) with balustrades and a wide hall with the huge stone statue of Kiliano di Limburg, founder of Castromediano house, of the chapel of St. Stefano with valuable paintings, and of the gallery with many statues of the typical stone from Lecce and with frescoed ceiling.

We must also notice the parish church of Our Lady, the Virgin Mary received into Heaven, built in the 15th century but rebuilt in the 17th and 18th centuries in Baroque forms and the three-aisle church in Seicento style of the ex convent of Dominican Fathers. The village was the birthplace of the great patriot Sigismondo Castromediano and the dialectal poet Giuseppe De Dominicis.

Leaving Cavallino we will reach Caprarica of Lecce and then Calimera, a village of Byzantine age, which together with the communes of Martano, Martignano, Zollino, Sternatia, Soleto, Corigliano d'Otranto, Melpignano and Castrignano dei Greci belongs to what remains of Salentine Grecia where few people still understand and speak the griko. It has got the parish church of St. Brizio of the 17th century, the chapel of the Crucified, the small church of St.

Alimini Lakes

Anthony, the small temple of St. Brizio, the church of the Madonna of Costantinopoli and the chapel of the Immaculate. Some hundreds of metres far from the village, near the cemetery, in the small church of St. Vito we find the famous pierced stone, that is a menanthol, through which people of any build pass for magic-propitiatory aims. Finally, in the parks there is the marble "stele" (a marble slab with inscriptions) of the 4th century BC., given as a gift by Athens to Calimera in memory of their common origins.

If we go on towards the Adriatic coast we will stop at Melendugno which was built in the 11th and perhaps its population increased owing to the refugees from Pasulo hamlet, destroyed by the Turks. In its territory there are "Placa" and "Guargulante" dolmens, both of them with a large covering slab in seven metres of perimeter. The village has got the small castle of D'Amelj family and the parish church, both of the 16th century, transformed into Baroque style in the following century. Near the village we find the small church of St. Niceta. Melendugno's resorts are: Roca (prehistorical and Messapian centre), San Foca, Torre dell'Orso and Torre Sant'Andrea, with remains of coastal fortifications and basilian lauras(a kind of monasteries).

Our way can go on towards Martano, whose old part keeps a castle and Baroque palaces.

Then we will stop at Carpignano, perhaps a centre of Roman origin which in the Middle Ages developed around the hypogeal (underground) crypt of Saints Marina and Cristina, endowed with beautiful

frescoes which are hardly previous to the year one thousand, dated and signed by Eustazio and Teofilatto painters, coming from the abbey of St. Nicola of Casole, near Otranto, where the Italo-Greek pictorial school flourished. We must also notice in Carpignano the Baroque parish church and Orsini palace, with a precious porch flanked with columns. Near the village, we also find the sanctuary of St. Mary of the Cave of the 16th century, later changed.

If we leave this village, we will arrive in Otranto, a town of very ancient origins, which was at first Messapian, then Greek, then Roman. For its strategic position, it was an important centre during the Byzantine age and, successively, in Norman, Angevin and Aragonese ages till 1480, when it was sacked by the Turks who slaughtered the population. Since then Otranto has no longer recovered from it, but it is rich in memories, monuments such as: the small frescoed Byzantine church of St. Peter, the Romanesque cathedral (12th century), famous for its floor mosaic by Pantaleone, a monk of the nearby, but dilapidated abbey of St. Nicola of Casole, which in the Middle Ages was an active centre of spirituality and a meeting point between the western and eastern cultures. This mosaic surprises and charms for its narration, for the synthesis of classical-medieval knowledge which does not fail to integrate itself with biblical events of knights and of life of man in Salento in the 12th century. Interesting is the crypt of this temple, a self-accomplished church supported by column with poly-

On previous page: the stretch of coast of Sant'Andrea and the small Byzantine church of St. Peter in Otranto

Otranto, a particular view of the Castle, the front and the nave of the Cathedral

style capitals, clearly taking their origins from churches and monuments of previous age.

In Otranto we must notice the mighty pentagonal castle, ordered to be built by Ferdinand I of Aragon on a previous fortified structure of the Norman-Swabian period. The castle is what remains of the walls fortified with ramparts which still seem to surround the old part of the town, characteristic for its buildings and narrow and winding streets.

Now Otranto is a famous resort, equipped with hotels, campings, structures such as: "Valtur" and "Serra degli Alimini", welcoming beaches and woods.

Going on along the Adriatic coast road we will find Santa Cesarea Terme, a renowned seaside resort, famous for its thermal baths rich in salt-iodic-sulphureous water and radio-active mud-baths, equipped with good hotel facilities and buildings of eclectic taste (19th-20th centuries). In its territory the human presence has been witnessed since the middle Palaeolithic age. There is a menhir and along the high and indented coast leading to Castro, there has been the discovery

Castro

of the prehistorical caves of Romanelli, Zinzulusa and Porto Badisco. Of probable Greek origin, Castro developed during the Roman age and it was an important episcopal seat since 682. The place was tormented and more times destroyed by the Turks. The village, which rises high on the sea, is endowed with building fortifications and a castle built in 1572, but later changed. Interesting is the Cathedral of the 12th century, built on the area of a previous Byzantine temple of two centuries before. In spite of restorations, this church still keeps the Romanesque plan.

Now we are in the territory of Capo di Leuca, where we find the pleasant centre of Santa Maria of Leuca which, originally Messapian, became later Roman and it is supposed to have been one of the first site where Christianity arrived. A coveted seaside resort, here between the end of the 19th century and the beginning of our century, delightful buildings of eclectic style, summer residences of the lords of the province were achieved.

On the extreme headland of Apulia that is Capo fo Santa Maria ofi Leuca, rises the famous sanctuary de Finibus Terrae rebuilt in 1720 and restored in 1835. This sanctuary, devoted to the Virgin of Leuca, destination for a lot of pilgrims, was the most devastated place by the Turks. The village, which is a place of mariners and boats navigation, is equipped with modern hotels, a modern Neo Romanesque parish church and, in the hinterland, with rupestrian (rocky) settlements.

San Cesario di Lecce, Villa Terragno

At a short distance from Leuca we find Tricase which, risen in Medieval Age, increased the inhabitants with the refugees from the nearby hamlets which were destroyed in the 15th century. An important monument in the village is the castle of the 14th century, restored in the 17th century, now seat of the Commune and schools. Interesting is the parish church in Cinquecento style, widely changed in 1770, as well as the church of St. Michele Arcangelo (1624) and the Baroque church of St. Domenico. In the territory of Tricase we find the Basilian crypt called of Gonfalone.

Of tourist interest are the Serra and Marina of Tricase.

If we go on, we will reach Ugento, a famous agricultural centre which was inhabited in prehistorical age and it became important in Messapian and Roman Age. It declined in Byzantine Age, it suffered various ravages, above all on the part of the Turks. The village had been an Episcopal seat since the 6th century; in 1818 it widened with its annexation to the dioceses of Alessano-Leuca.

Among the town monuments we find two menhirs, megalithic walls, the castle of the 14th century rebuilt in the 18th century, as well as other buildings destroyed by the Turks such as: the Episcopal palace and the cathedral. In the territory there are various basilian crypts, the most famous of which is that of the Crucified, and the small Romanesque church of St. Mary of Casale.

Before arriving at the villages of the coastline and

of the Ionic hinterland we will stop for a little time at Patù which was probably founded by the refugees from Vereto who had escaped from the destruction of their hamlet, on the part of the Saracens, in the 9th century. The place was inhabited by the Messapians and it preserves the ancient megalithic monument called Centopietre (one hundred stones), of controversial origin. Opposite to this rectangular monument, in the shape, of a small temple, there is the remarkable castle, endowed with strong embattled towers of the 16th century.

After leaving Patù, we can go to Taurisano, probably known during the Roman Age. The palace has brought to light many archaeological finds of various ages, above all of the Medieval one. The village has got the interesting Roman church of St. Mary della Strada (of Road), the ducal residence and the parish church of the last century. In Taurisano the famous philosopher Giulio Cesare Vanini was born in 1585, whom the religious intolerance made him burn alive in Tolosa.

Now we can go the extreme ramification of the peninsula of Salento in order to reach Casarano, originally Byzantine, now an important place for agriculture and shoe industry. In the suburb of Casaranello, the original centre of the village, we find the church of St. Mary della Croce (of Cross), begun to be built in the 5th century AD. and then kept on in the protoRomanesque period. This temple is decorated with Byzantine mosaics and frescoes of various periods, but not following the 13th century ages.

Even the crypt of St. Costantina, in the neighbourhood of Casaranello, which keeps frescoes of the 16th and 17th centuries still belongs to the Byzantine Age. Besides, we must also notice the parish church of Our Lady of the Annunciation (1712), the spire of St. John the Almoner (1850) and the church of the Madonna of the Bell, of Byzantine origin but rebuilt in Baroque style in 1639. Casarano was the birthplace of Pietro Tomacelli who, in 1389, was elected as pope with the name of Bonifacio IX.

Going out of Casarano, after some kilometres, we will find Parabita, where the human presence has been witnessed since the Palaeolithic period, as it is proved by finds discovered in the "Cave of Venuses". Nevertheless, the village became a built-up area in Messapian Age with the name Bavota. Two small bone statues of women, decorated pebbles and graffiti come from the "Cave of Venuses", but Parabita was also such an important basilian centre, that in its territory a monolithic painting representing the Virgin was found by chance and, for this reason, the Modern Neo-Romanesque Sanctuary of the Madonna della Coltura (of the Cultivation) was built. Other crypts representing sacred images are in the territory of Parabita such as: that of Cirlicì, St. Eleuterio, of the Madonna of the Carotto, all of them without any frescoes. In the village we must notice small ancient palaces, the castle of Castriota family, of the 16th century, the ex convents of Dominicans and Alcantarini.

In the middle part of Salento there is Maglie, whose origin is uncertain, even it is supposed to belong to Byzantine Age. The village is a famous agricultural, industrial and manufacturing centre. Once in Maglie there was a church with Byzantine chapels, but in Baroque Age the place was renewed, and some palaces in the old part of the town bear witness to it such as: Capece palace. The Mother church, devoted to St. Nicola, dates back to the 18th century, a year before the building of the temple of the Graces, and contemporary to the churches of Our Lady of Sorrows and of the Conventual Friars. In Maglie some menhirs are still preserved.

Not so far from Maglie is Poggiardo risen in Medieval Age, around the half of the 12th century, when the inhabitants of Vaste sought refuge here after escaping from the Norman soldiery of Guglielmo il Malo.

The village was an episcopal seat from 1537 to 1818 and the bishop of Castro resided here. The place bears witness to the settlement of Basilian crypts, of which important frescoes remain, and it has the majestic ducal palace built in Angevin period. The parish church is in a simple style. (1728).

The nearby hamlet of Vaste is an important archaeological station of Messapian Age and iconodulo (following the worship for sacred images) monachism of which the crypt of the Saints Stefani remains.

At about one kilometre from Maglie we will find Muro Leccese, whose site bears witness to the presence of the Megalithic and Messapian Age, of which some parts of the mighty boundary walls remain. In the village we will admire the small Medieval church of St. Marina, the parish church, the church of the Immaculate, as well as the castle of the most Protonoble, the church and the convent of Dominicans.

Gallipoli, the Ravelin and the Castle,
and the Hellenistic fountain

From Muro we will reach Soleto, where man has existed since the prehistory and this is proved by a menhir and varied lithium industry. Soleto was an important Messapian and Byzantine centre, but it declined in Roman Age. Interesting is its old part where we find buildings belonging to the 14th –16th centuries.

The small Romanesque church of St. Stefano dates back to 1347, rebuilt on a previous temple and rich in Byzantine frescoes and others always referring to Byzantine style which can be attributed to the Italo-Greek pictorial school of St. Nicola of Casale. In 1397 the famous bell tower was built in flowery-gothic style. This "Guglia" (Spire) ordered to be built by Raimondello Orsini del Balzo is the unique work of art by the architect Francesco Colaci from Surbo that we know. We must also notice the Baroque parish church (1770-1783), the monastery of Clarisses and the ancient convent of the Minorites. Soleto was the birthplace of Matteo Tafuri, a scholar, a magician and a necromancer of the 16th century who became famous all over the Europe.

Caterina" for the Gothic elegance. Even the tombs of Raimondello and Giovanni Antonio Orsini del Balzo are of Gothic taste. Finally we must notice the parish church of the Saints Peter and Paul of the 17th century, the ancient church of Souls, the civic museum "Pietro Cavoti" endowed with valuable paintings. In Galatina the phenomenon of "tarantate" is still alive, women who usually dance obsessively and frenetically in the chapel of St. Paul to free themselves from effect of the bite of the tarantola (a big spider).

Now let's go near to the Ionic hinterland in order to find Galatone, centre of High Medieval period, whose economy is based on agriculture even if it has also some small industry. The village was fortified with walls after the year one thousand, but it suffered sacks and ravages on the part of the Turks. It has got part of the castle and it consists in an imposing square embattled tower changed in the 16th century; the village still keeps some parts of the walls and a pretty door in Cinquecento style. Interesting is the Baroque church of St. Sebastiano (18th century), but a real work of art is the church of the Crucified of Mercy (1696-110) with a Baroque plan with three orders which is decorated with a beautiful lacunar. The Major church (1574-1595) and the church of Dominicans (1612-1712), as well as the small church of St. Peter are in Baroque style.

In the neighbourhood of the village which was the birthplace of the famous humanist Antonio De Ferraris, called the Galateo (16th century) we can notice the ruins of the Norman castle of Fulcignano, the small basilian church of St. Nicola of Pergoleti and in the centre of the Town the small Romanesque church of Itria (12th century).

Gallipoli is reflected in the Ionian Sea, town of Messapian or Greek origin, which for its geographical position, always played a primary role and, therefore, it was contended and coveted by many conquerors of the lands of Salento. The "beautiful town" (from Greek: Kalepolis) rises on an island, but in the past , before the 17th century, it was linked with the dry land

Near here we find Galatina, a town of very ancient origins which developed in the Byzantine Middle Ages. It is an active centre for agriculture, trade and the manufactories. Between the 16th and the 18th centuries the town of Galatina developed, now having precious palaces such as: Gorgoni palace, Vernaleone palace, Venturi palace, and Galluccio-Mezio palace. Among the monuments stands out the gothic church of St. Caterina from Alessandria (1384-1391), though having Romanesque elements. The temple is rich in frescoes, among which some "allegories" and scenes from Apocalypse stand out; some detail of "Transito", of "Mercy" and the "Stories of St.

Nardò, le Quattro colonne (the Four Columns)

where since 1860 the new village has begun to be built. Powerful under the Roman domination, in 551 it became an episcopal seat, then a Byzantine stronghold and centre of Greek workship. Since 915, for over thirty years the town was under the domination of the Saracens, then the Normans succeeded them and after that, altogether it followed the destiny of Terra D'Otranto. The monuments of the "pearl of the Ionian Sea" are so many such as: the Hellenistic fountain (16th century), the Sanctuary of St. Mary of Canneto (cane field), the castle of the 16th century built on previous fortifications, the imposing town walls who surround the whole island, whose area was strongly influenced by the Arabs for its intricate streets and for the painted white house. Next to the blocks of buildings and the ones included in "corti" (courtyards) typical of the Mediterranean architecture, Gallipoli has got Baroque palaces among which we find: Ravenna palace, Tafuri palace, Venneri palace and Senape-De Pace palace.

Among so many churches we must point out the wonderful Baroque Cathedral devoted to St. Agata (1630-1696), decorated with so many valuable paintings, the church of Purity (17th century), rich in paintings and stuccoes, the church of St. Francesco from Assisi (17th-18th centuries) also famous for the statue of mal ladrone (bad thief), and, then, the church of St. Domenico (or of Rosario), the church of the Souls and that of the Crucified. Gallipoli, desired destination for many tourists and endowed with beaches, hotels and campings has got a good civic museum and a rich town library.

At some kilometres from Gallipoli rises Alezio, an important Messapian archaeological station where tombs with funeral equipment, coins and inscriptions have been brought to light. The village has the late Romanesque church of the Madonna of Lizza, where we can still admire some Byzantine frescoes.

The commune of Sannicola adjoins that of Alezio, where, opposite to Gallipoli, on a height we can discern the ruins of the Abbey of St. Mauro where, in spite of so many ruins, we will find frescoes of Byzantine Middle Ages.

If we keep going up towards the hinterland we will find Nardò, an important agricultural and manufacturing centre which was a flourishing Messapian centre and it was very important during the Byzantine and Norman period. Nardò suffered the trouble of feudal struggles, it suffered the incursions of the Turks, it was coveted by so many invaders but in the 17th century, together with Lecce, it lead the Anti-Spanish revolt which was then cruelly repressed trough bloodshed. The social revival of the village occurred during the Risorgimento when people took part in uprisings and joined Young Italy. The imposing cathedral belongs to the Middle Ages, rebuilt in 1721 and restored between 1892 and 1900. The church keeps the precious Black Christ Crucified, a wooden work of art of the 12th century, and many frescoes of the 12th and 15th centuries. The town is rich in Baroque palaces and churches among which there is the interesting temple of St. Domenico, changed in 1743; there are also the important churches of St. Joseph, of the Immaculate, of St. Teresa and of the Capuchins. We must remember, then, the palace of the "Prefecture" (1722), now seat of the magistrate's court, the "Guglia" (Spire) of the Immaculate (1769), the imposing castle (16th century) which now hosts the town hall, the Roman walls, the crypt of St. Anthony the Abbot and, along the coast, many defence towers and watch towers dating back to the 16th century.

After leaving Nardò we will go on for Copertino which rose around the year one thousand thanks to farmers coming from the nearby hamlets which had been destroyed by the Saracens. The village developed during the Byzantine domination and it widened so much under the Angevins that Charles D'Angiò raised the small town to earldom. Tristano of Chiaromonte, in 1430, surrounded it with walls and ramparts; in the 16th century Alfonso Castriota Scanderberg fortified the town again endowing it with embattled towers and he commissioned the local architect Evangelista Menga to build the mighty castle which still today surprises us for its structure and elegance. This fortress, dating back to 1540, is fortified with ramparts, has a trapezoidal form and it is surrounded by a wide moat.

Houses and palaces of various times, above all of the 18th century, represent the old part of Copertino, among whose monuments we must remember the Collegiata (St. Mary of Snow) rebuilt in 1707 on a 16th century temple. Then the sanctuary of St. Joseph from Copertino, a building of refined Baroque taste, belongs to 1754-58. In the neighbourhood of the village which is a famous agriculture centre, there is the ancient convent of the Grottella, more times changed and the crumbling convent of St. Nicola of Casole (1513).

At a short distance from Copertino we will find Leverano. In Leverano we must notice the parish church of 1603 and the contemporary convent of the Minorites. From Leverano we can reach Porto Cesareo where there are important monuments such as: an ancient archaeological station and a quadrangular tower of the 16th century, built like many other defensive buildings in order to defend the territory from Turkish and piratical incursions.

OMNIBUS, pubblicazione periodica quindicinale, anno II, n. 1 del 15 marzo 2001.
Autorizzazione del Tribunale di Lecce - Registro della Stampa n. 733 del 26. 5. 2000.

Direttore Responsabile: Lorenzo Capone

Capone Editore,
Via provinciale Lecce-Cavallino, km. 1,250 - Lecce
Tel. 0832612618 - 0832611877(fax)

E. mail: l.capone@telematicaitalia.it

Translated by Letizia Ferrari

Le foto delle pagine 5, 6, 7, 8, 9, 10, 11, 12, 13, 14, 15, 17, 18, 19, 20, 21, 22, 23, 25, 27, 28, 29, 30, 31, 32, 33, 34, 36, 38, 39, 40, 41, 46, 47, 49, 50, 51, 53, 54, 58, 59, 62, 63, 89, 90, 91, 92, 93, 94, 95, 99, sono dello Studio Cautillo di Foggia; quelle delle pagine 60, 61, 65, 77, 79, 80, 83, 97, 98, 101, 103, 104, 105, 106, 107, 109, 110, 111, 112, 113, 114, 115, 117, 118, 119, 120, sono di Pierluigi Bolognini; quelle delle pagine 24, 55, 64, 67, 68, 69, 70, 71, 74, 81, 85 sono di Annamaria Contenti; quelle delle pagine 72, 73, 78, 86, 100, sono di Claudio Longo; quelle delle pagine 37, 44, 45, sono di Ornella Grima; la foto aerea di pag. 35 è di Gianni Bezzato e quella di pagina 56 di Fernando Mezzina.

Finito di stampare nel mese di gennaio 2001 dalla AGM di Lecce